C000090830

# CHERWELL VALLEY RAILWAY

## THE SOCIAL HISTORY OF AN OXFORDSHIRE RAILWAY

# CHERWELL VALLEY RAILWAY

## THE SOCIAL HISTORY OF AN OXFORDSHIRE RAILWAY

*Peter Allen*

TEMPUS

First published 1999
First paperback edition 1999

PUBLISHED IN THE UNITED KINGDOM BY:

Tempus Publishing Ltd
The Mill, Brimscombe Port
Stroud, Gloucestershire GL5 2QG

PUBLISHED IN THE UNITED STATES OF AMERICA BY:

Tempus Publishing Inc.
2 Cumberland Street
Charleston, SC 29401

Tempus books are available in France, Germany and Belgium
from the following addresses:

| Tempus Publishing Group | Tempus Publishing Group | Tempus Publishing Group |
| --- | --- | --- |
| 21 Avenue de la République | Gustav-Adolf-Straße 3 | Place de L'Alma 4/5 |
| 37300 Joué-lès-Tours | 99084 Erfurt | 1200 Brussels |
| FRANCE | GERMANY | BELGIUM |

© Peter Allen, 1999

The right of Peter Allen to be identified as the Author
of this work has been asserted by him in accordance with the
Copyrights, Designs and Patents Act 1988.

All rights reserved. No part of this book may be reprinted or reproduced or utilised in
any form or by any electronic, mechanical or other means, now known or hereafter
invented, including photocopying and recording, or in any information storage or
retrieval system, without the permission in writing from the Publishers.

British Library Cataloguing in Publication Data.
A catalogue record for this book is available from the British Library.

ISBN 0 7524 1718 5

Typesetting and origination by Tempus Publishing.
PRINTED AND BOUND IN GREAT BRITAIN.

# Contents

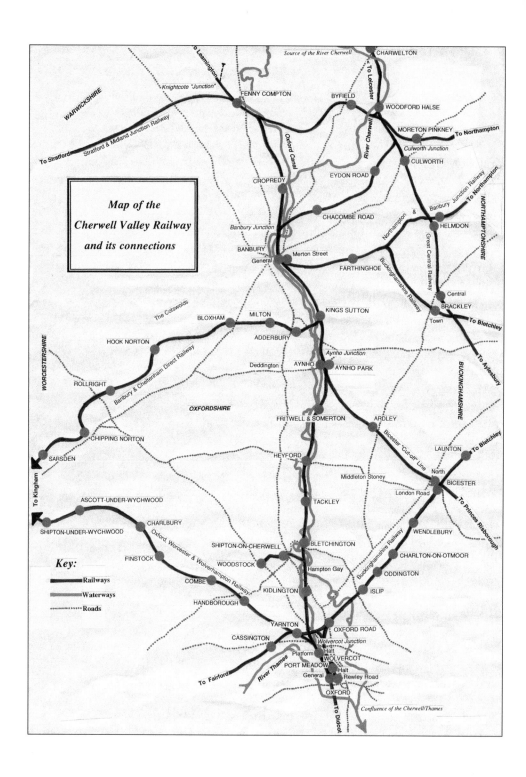

Map of the
Cherwell Valley Railway
and its connections

# 1   Setting the scene

The 'Three Shires Stone' marks the point where the counties of Northamptonshire, Warwickshire and Oxfordshire meet. The neighbouring villages of Boddington, Fenny Compton and Claydon are actually located in each of the respective counties. This region lies between Southern England and Industrial Midlands, yet is neither one nor the other, instead possessing a character of its own. It is in Northamptonshire, where the land rises to over six hundred feet above sea level, that the stripling River Cherwell has its source, at Charwelton, beyond Woodford Halse. Despite originating in that county, the Cherwell is justly known far and wide as an Oxfordshire river, for it quickly drops over the county boundary to make the latter shire its home.

The River Cherwell flows west into Oxfordshire, past the village of Cropredy, where it is now only a little over three hundred feet above sea level. During the English Civil War – on 29 June, 1644 – Royalist and Parliamentary troops fought here in the Battle of Cropredy Bridge. The river turns south at this point towards its ultimate destination some thirty miles distant. In its upper valley, the Cherwell threads its way through a 'redland' landscape which typifies north Oxfordshire. This is limestone country, but there are extensive iron deposits in the ground – a useful mineral, the ore has long been quarried in surface mines. The soil is also productive for farming, and in 1809 Arthur Young credited it with being 'adapted to every plant that can be trusted to it.'

Before it has got very far on its journey, the river has reached Banbury, the market town famous for its cross. In the twelfth century, the town belonged to the Bishops of Lincoln, one of whom had the town rebuilt and a castle constructed. With a rich agricultural hinterland, Banbury has long been a natural market for the region, and several roads converge on the place. The town was also renowned for ale, cheese and 'Banbury Cakes'; textiles were made too, including woollen cloth and plush. In the nineteenth century Banbury developed industrially with the manufacture of machinery. By mid-century, Bernhard Samuelson had set up the Britannia Engineering Works where various items of farm machinery were made.

For about six miles southwards from Banbury, the river forms the boundary between the counties of its birth and adoption, with Oxfordshire on its west bank and Northamptonshire on its east. On both sides of the river there are farms and pretty stone cottages, many constructed from the golden-brown local marlstone. There are some attractive villages, whose fine churches are celebrated in verse: 'Adderbury for length, Bloxham for strength, and Kings Sutton for beauty.' Adderbury (Oxon), a mile or so from the river, is a large village which once had the right to hold markets. Kings Sutton (Northants), close by the river, is a smaller village with its own supply of spring water, which in its day vied with that at Leamington Spa.

The stripling River Cherwell passes under the A361 near its source at Charwelton.

King's Sutton church, celebrated in rhyme for its 'beauty' – and its tall spire.

A couple of miles further south, on opposite banks of the river again, are the villages of Deddington (Oxon) and Aynho (Northants). At the time of Domesday, Deddington was twice as wealthy as Banbury. It had a castle, a town hall, a market place and regular fairs, such as the 'Pudding Pie Fair' held in November of each year. Overtaken by Banbury in the Middle Ages, Deddington lapsed until by the nineteenth century it was just another village. Across the river, Aynho is perhaps best known for its park, although it is also the most south-westerly of Northamptonshire's villages. It is at this point that the river ceases to mark the county boundary, which swings off to the east. Now, both banks of the river become Oxfordshire's.

A change in the countryside reflects the changing geology from this point, as the limestone deteriorates into a rubbly grey Cornbrash. However, agriculture remains the dominant activity and many of the villages are still picturesque and historical. The names of some of the villages have ancient origins, such as Somerton, which (with Fritwell and Souldern) may have been used as summer pastureland in Saxon times. Further south on the Cherwell, Heyford is another such place, its name suggesting that here was a ford across the river, which was used particularly at the time of the hay harvest. Later on, Heyford had a bridge and a market square, where a 'Root Show' was held in September of each year.

The Oxfordshire Cotswolds climb to over six hundred feet westwards from the Cherwell, which is now in its lower valley. In ancient times the royal forest of Wychwood covered an extensive tract of land on this side of the river, but later it contracted considerably. Nevertheless, perhaps as a legacy of earlier days, much

Lower Heyford, *c*.1910. After surveying this area in the 1840s, Brunel decided to build the GWR line around the village rather than through it as it would be cheaper. (Courtesy of Kingfisher Postcards)

of this part of central Oxfordshire is given over to parkland. To the east of the river, there are parks at Bletchingdon, Kirtlington (home of the Dashwood family) and Middleton Stoney (residence of the Earls of Jersey). To the west are Rousham (home of the Cottrell-Dormer family), Tackley, Glympton and – most famous of them all – Blenheim Park (residence of the Dukes of Marlborough) at Woodstock.

Woodstock was a royal manor at the time of Domesday and at Woodstock Park medieval kings patronized a hunting lodge built by Henry I in the twelfth century. His grandson, Henry II, granted the town a market, with a fair added later. Henry II frequently visited Woodstock to indulge in an illicit romance with 'Fair Rosamund' (Rosamund Clifford), his mistress. Woodstock, long noted for its leather trade, especially glove-making, is a town of Cotswold stone buildings, many of them dating from the eighteenth century. It was at this period that the splendid palace and park were constructed for John Churchill, 1st Duke of Marlborough, in recognition of his victory over the French at the Battle of Blenheim in 1704.

On the opposite side of the valley are villages like Kirtlington, Bletchingdon, Hampton Poyle and Hampton Gay. Of them all, Kirtlington has the most distinguished history, as a one-time Saxon royal manor and later as a wealthy medieval parish. The other villages are probably best remembered as centres of unrest associated with the sixteenth-century enclosure movement. The poor cottagers, deprived of their livelihoods by a change from arable to sheep farming in the area, threatened violent protest in 1596, but to no avail. In the end they were forced off the land, resulting in depopulation of some villages. Hampton Gay became a 'deserted village', its ruined cottages watched over by a lonely little church.

Nearing the end of its journey, the river here creates a wide flood plain in its circuitous course. According to a rhyme, 'Cherwell winds with devious coil, round Hampton Gay and Hampton Poyle.' It skirts around the older part of the village of Kidlington, close to the church noted for its tall steeple, which is something of a local landmark. Thomas Beecham, founder of the pill firm, came to live at Kidlington in 1840. The Cherwell continues east towards the great marsh of Ot Moor, to meet the River Ray (a lesser stream) at Islip, before turning south again. It drops below the two hundred feet level onto the flat plain of Oxford Clay, overlain in places with gravel terraces. Less flood-prone, these afford suitable sites for settlement.

On one of these gravel terraces, long ago, the city of Oxford had its origins. However, tradition claims that it was not founded until AD 727, when St Frideswide had a monastery built and a walled town developed. The university, which most people associate with Oxford, only began in the twelfth century with the influx of scholars and teachers, and the first colleges were not built until the late thirteenth century. During the Civil War, in 1642, King Charles I made his headquarters at Oxford but was obliged to surrender the city in 1646. The growth of Oxford as a 'town' was heavily dependent on 'gown', and for most of the city's history the latter was dominant although this did not prevent a conflict of interests at times.

The premises of S.W. Smith, carpenter, wheelwright and undertaker, Lyne Road, Kidlington, *c*.1905. (Courtesy of Kingfisher Postcards)

Martyrs Memorial, St Giles, Oxford, *c*.1910. The memorial was built to commemorate the Protestant bishops Cranmer, Latimer and Ridley, who were burned at the stake nearby during the reign of Queen Mary. (Courtesy of Kingfisher Postcards)

The River Thames flows through Oxford, where prehistoric trackways – on which cattle were driven – forded the stream, and so gave the city its name. At Oxford, too, the River Cherwell loses its separate identity, for it is but a tributary of the former river. It has journeyed from the hills of Northamptonshire to the vale of Oxfordshire; it has passed all manner of settlements between the market town of Banbury and the university city of Oxford; it has helped to create much of the scenery, and to shape the lives of the people, along its route. At Oxford the Cherwell makes its way through the University Parks and, in Christ Church Meadow south-east of the city centre, its waters are swallowed up by the Thames and carried off to London.

From Saxon times through to the nineteenth century, the River Thames was a principal transport route from Oxford to London and the sea. 'Sea coal' was the most important commodity carried on the river, being brought to Oxford from Newcastle via London. However, the waterway was notoriously unreliable: apart from the perennial difficulties of flood and drought, there were problems with mills and weirs throughout the Middle Ages. The first in a series of Acts of Parliament was passed in 1605, by means of which navigation on the river was gradually improved, but it was often obstructed temporarily. In 1793 boats were taking two months to get from London to Oxford and, on such occasions, the price of commodities increased in Oxford.

The River Cherwell and its tributaries have never really been navigable although there have been attempts to make them so. During the Civil War period, in 1644, the Royalists considered improving the Cherwell, Ray and Otmoor streams in order to bring supplies to Oxford from the north-east. Orders were issued that, 'Bridges, Mills, Weirs and other impediments upon the said rivers ... be removed or altered according as the necessity of the service shall require.' Furthermore, various officials were ordered to 'aid and assist ... in passing Carts, Teams, Boats and Workmen, and to contribute their help in all such matters.' However, there is no evidence to indicate that any work was actually undertaken towards this end.

Later in the seventeenth century, Andrew Yarranton, who had served in the Parliamentary army, proposed two schemes for making the Cherwell navigable. One – costed at £2,500 - was to open up the river as far as Aynho; the other – at £10,000 – was to make the river navigable through to Banbury, with a wagon connection overland to the Warwickshire Avon. The second, and more ambitious scheme, would thus afford a link between the Thames and the Severn. There is evidence to suggest that the latter scheme may have been attempted, since at least one Banbury merchant, a certain Sanderson Miller, is on record as having brought his goods from Oxford to Banbury, in flat-bottomed boats, in the early eighteenth century.

Two experimental trips were made from Oxford, up the rivers Cherwell and Ray, in 1764. The first, in January, was with a barge loaded with coal, which travelled through Islip to Lower Arncott bridge on the River Ray, the coal being taken on to Ambrosden Park in wheelbarrows! The barge returned to Oxford, loaded with barley, two days later. The second trip, in February, was over the same route but with an empty vessel which went 'to make observations on that new discovered passage', and got as far as Bicester. Like the Thames, the Cherwell was an unreliable navigation, however, and although the stream was still accessible to boats as far as Shipton in 1777, by this date the river was no longer navigable up to Banbury.

It was the unreliable nature of navigation on rivers like the Cherwell and the Thames that inspired people to contemplate the construction of artificial waterways in the eighteenth century. Thus the Oxford Canal came into being as a vital link between the coalfields of the industrial Midlands and London. The instigator of this project was Sir Roger Newdigate of Coventry, who visited Banbury in 1768 to promote the idea. James Brindley, the celebrated canal engineer, surveyed the route and prepared plans for the canal, which received Royal Assent in April 1769. Brindley died in 1772 but construction progressed rapidly and the canal was opened from Coventry to Banbury on 30 March, 1778, when 200 tons of coal arrived at the town's wharf.

Shortage of money held up progress south of Banbury, and the poor suffered for want of cheap coal. In winter there was great distress at places like Heyford because there were 'no materials by which the poor could procure even a wretched fire'. To economize on construction, at Heyford the canal occupied the course of the Cherwell (the river being diverted into a new channel) and at Shipton the canal and river merged into a single waterway for a mile. At last, on 1 January, 1790, the canal was opened from Banbury to Oxford where, on that New Year's Day, a fleet of boats arrived, bringing in coal, corn and other goods. At

Lower Heyford, *c*.1910. At the annual 'Root Show' here in 1848, speakers joked about the delay in building the Oxford & Rugby Railway. (Courtesy of Kingfisher Postcards)

the city basin, Warwickshire coal was available for only 1s 4d per cwt. – half its previous price.

Reductions in the price of coal were effected all along the canal, benefiting domestic users and bringing industrial potential to the Cherwell valley. The canal became an artery of industry, particularly for heavy and bulky commodities, and wharves were opened at places like Cropredy, Adderbury, Heyford and Enslow, near Kirtlington. The canal also served traditional rural needs, carrying agricultural goods on boats like John Weaving's market boat, which carried produce between Oxford and Banbury, calling at villages *en route*. However, problems still arose; as Arthur Young noted, in the hot summers of 1790 and 1791, the boats were 'nearly on dry land', while in the freezing winter of 1795 there was a ten week stoppage because of ice.

The alternative means of transport, road travel, was in the same state at this date: poor but improving. At the beginning of the eighteenth century Oxfordshire's roads were little better than the prehistoric trackways they had succeeded, being notoriously bad and almost impassable in winter. For villagers in the mid-Cherwell valley, the journey to market in Oxford could mean a three-day round trip by wagon at this time. Both Oxford and Banbury were important route centres for what roads there were in this period, gaining improved communications under the early turnpike schemes. By 1720, the road from London to Oxford had been almost completely turnpiked, and that from Oxford to Banbury was turnpiked under an Act of 1755.

Turnpikes encouraged stage coaches to join the carriers' wagons on the roads. The first stage coach service Oxford had was that to London, used by Anthony Wood in 1667 when it ran thrice weekly and took two days each way with an overnight stop at Beaconsfield. By the early nineteenth century the time for the same journey had been cut to six or seven hours, and similar improvements had been effected on main roads throughout Oxfordshire. In 1809, Arthur Young again – a confirmed coach traveller – wrote that he detected 'a noble change' in the county's roads. The turnpikes, he said, were 'very good and where gravel is to be had, excellent.' As a result, Oxford and Banbury grew rapidly into major coaching centres.

Oxford's central position in southern England made it a focal point for coach services, and here the inns afforded temporary stopping places to change horses and crews. The city had several excellent coaching inns, such as the Roebuck and the Star in Cornmarket Street, and the Mitre and the Angel in the High Street. An old coach guard, William Bazand, claimed that around 1820 no fewer than seventy-three separate coaches a day called at Oxford inns, connecting with destinations at all points of the compass. Of the Angel he wrote: 'I don't think you could witness in any other town in the kingdom the same number of coaches standing before an hotel, and nine out of ten to start at the same time' – that is, at eight in the morning.

Seven turnpike roads linked Banbury with neighbouring towns, and the earliest regular coach service of which there is any record was to Birmingham in 1731. By

Banbury Cross, the famous landmark in the centre of the North Oxfordshire town. This cross, dating from *c.*1860, replaced a medieval cross destroyed by the Puritans in around 1600.

1760 there was a service to the capital from the Three Tuns in Banbury, and other services to London were established later. In 1830 some forty-seven coaches a week served Banbury, many working from the Flying Horse, an inn kept by John Drinkwater, a partner in the Birmingham-Oxford 'Regulator' coach. The peak year for Banbury's coach services was 1836, at which time most coaches called at the White Lion. At this date, the weekly service of coaches was twenty-two to London (reached in just seven and a half hours by the fastest coach), nineteen to Birmingham and twelve to Oxford.

Local transport needs were met in other ways in this period. The coach route from Oxford to Banbury then lay through Woodstock, and John Drinkwater operated a twice-weekly service by this route from 1792. It started from the Catherine Wheel at Banbury at 1.00 p.m. and ran to the New Inn at Oxford, arriving in the evening. On the canal, John Weaving operated his weekly market boat (which also carried passengers) between Banbury and Oxford, contriving to arrive in each place on market days, Thursday and Saturday respectively. The market towns also attracted hundreds of carriers' carts, especially Banbury, which was known as 'the metropolis of the carriers' carts' On market day, up to 300 carriers attended Banbury market.

The state of transport in the area was described by the contemporary local historian William Wing. The roads were 'alive nearly every hour of the day and some of the hours of the night with the elegantly-painted, well-horsed, four-in-hand stage coaches and mail coaches'. On the roads too, heavy, long distance, eight-horse wagons were transporting goods by day and by night, while covered carts, travelling from farm to farm, collected butter, pork and poultry and thus supplemented the canal's market boat service. Also on the canal, boats were conveying cargoes of coal, timber and corn from wharf to wharf. This, then, was the scene in Oxfordshire in the mid-nineteenth century.

Of course, the railway age was well under way by this date and there were already trunk routes reaching out from London. It was in 1844 that a railway first reached the foot of the Cherwell Valley at Oxford. A terminus station was built near Folly Bridge, on the south bank of the River Thames and the west side of the Abingdon turnpike road. The train service commenced on Wednesday 12 June in that year, when a branch line to Oxford was opened for public use. It connected the city with a main line at Didcot, just under ten miles away. The securing of this toehold in Oxford had the effect of making the Cherwell Valley a 'front line' in the railway rivalries of the time.

The mid-1840s was a complicated period in Britain's railway history, now known as the second 'Railway Mania'. Some indication of its extent is evident in the total railway mileage authorized in these years: in 1843 the figure was less than 100 miles; in 1844 it exceeded 800 miles; in 1845 it was nearly 3,000; and in 1846 it was over 4,500 miles. These lines were proposed by private railway companies, independent and competing with one another, and sometimes with different *modus operandi*, including the construction of tracks of different widths, which often brought them into conflict. It was in this period of 'mania' that the railway came to the Cherwell Valley.

# 2 Railway rivalry

Oxford and the Cherwell Valley lay in an area bounded by two major railway lines radiating from London, one to Bristol and the other to Birmingham. The latter was the London & Birmingham (later the London & North Western) Railway, engineered by the famous father and son George and Robert Stephenson using the narrow gauge of track. The former was the Great Western Railway, built by the equally celebrated engineer Isambard Kingdom Brunel using the broad gauge of track. The Oxford branch was itself a broad-gauge protégé, and the GWR could not wait to add a northward extension.

Even before their first train had arrived in Oxford, the directors of the GWR were planning to extend their branch line from the south into the virgin territory beyond the city. The Cherwell Valley was the route of their proposed 'Oxford & Rugby Railway'. At this time, Rugby – famous for its public school – was a town of over 4,000 inhabitants. It had the right to hold no fewer than eleven annual fairs and a large cattle market each Saturday. By 1840 it had become an important railway centre and 'the gate to the whole of the north', hence the GWR's interest in capturing the territory from Oxford to Rugby.

However, the L&B Railway, realizing that whichever company staked the first claim to the area would have the advantage in exploiting it, projected its own line through Oxfordshire from the east. It planned to build a 'London, Worcester & South Staffordshire Railway' from its London-Birmingham line at Tring to Wolverhampton. The proposed route was via Aylesbury, Bicester, Banbury, Evesham and Worcester, with branches from Bicester to Oxford and from north of Oxford to Rugby. It was obvious that the branches formed an alternative Oxford and Rugby railway – war was declared!

As a result of these competing claims to territory, what became known as the 'Battle of the Gauges' was also fought, since the two companies used tracks of different widths. The two issues – of territory and gauge – were inextricably linked and the final outcome depended upon their resolution. The GWR had an initial advantage, given their toe-hold in Oxford, but the L&B could respond by playing up the problems presented by the 'break of gauge' that arose where the broad-gauge tracks met other lines built to the more common narrow gauge, (or 'standard gauge', as it eventually became known).

Several things were necessary before any railway could be built: the support of local public opinion, access to financial capital and an enabling Act of Parliament. In pursuit of these objectives, public and private meetings were held in Oxford and Banbury to sound out the inhabitants' views. The GWR fired the first shot in trying to gain the confidence of influential members of each community. The local press reported a private meeting held at the Angel Hotel in Oxford as early as Tuesday 14 May 1844, to which plans for northward extensions of the GWR were put.

It was reported that the meeting was attended by 'many of the most influential persons in the University, city, and county'. It was addressed by Charles A. Saunders (secretary to the GWR), Frederick P. Barlow (a director), and Isambard K. Brunel (the engineer). Mr Barlow spoke first and explained the GWR's proposal to extend the Oxford branch to Banbury, with two continuations thence 'in one direction to Rugby, and in another to Worcester'. (The latter proposal was dropped in September 1844, however, in favour of a more direct line.)

Mr Barlow stated that the GWR 'were perfectly sincere in their proposals, as it would be for their own benefit' and stated that the company would raise the capital needed for the line from shares 'for which they would offer a guarantee from three to four per cent'. Mr Brunel's speech was intended to reassure the meeting on the question of the break of gauge, and he claimed that the cost of transferring from one gauge to another at Rugby 'would be so immaterial that it would not make a difference of 2d a ton in regard to the carriage of goods'. Both men's claims were actually somewhat dubious!

Very little controversy ensued at this private meeting and it is probable that Barlow and Brunel were preaching to known sympathizers in this rather select group. Nevertheless, the GWR was taken to task afterwards, by hostile letters in *Jackson's Oxford Journal,* over the manner in which the meeting had been arranged. One letter alleged it had not been 'a fair assemblage of influential inhabitants', only of a number of gentlemen 'brought together by special invitations, such invitations having been sent only to those who were supposed to be favourable to the project.' The letter went on to describe the GWR's private meeting as a 'hole and corner way of doing business', and urged caution before accepting either the broad or narrow gauge proposals, considering 'the vast influence the contemplated Rail will have on the trade of the town and health of its inhabitants'. The writer implored 'all, whether of University or City, to pause before they take either Company by the hand', and was signed 'Anti-Mania'. As the identity of the writer is not known, it is difficult to be sure of his precise motives in putting pen to paper. Further letters on the matter were published in subsequent weeks.

The same newspaper which carried the letter also published a petition against the GWR's broad-gauge line and in favour of the L&B's narrow-gauge line. It was signed by approximately 300 persons, the 'inhabitants of Banbury' and the 'owners or occupiers of property' along the proposed line of railway. Perhaps not surprisingly, therefore, the next meeting was held in Banbury and was on this occasion a public meeting. It was held in the British School Room on Friday 5 July 1844 and was presided over by Mr J.A. Gillett, a local banker, with more than 600 people in attendance.

Different railway projects for the area were put to the meeting, each presented by representatives of the particular schemes. This time, the L&B were represented by Messrs George and Robert Stephenson – the latter had been seen surveying in the district during the spring. Messrs Brunel, Saunders and Barlow again spoke for the GWR. In his speech, Mr Barlow exercised a degree of license: referring to the journey he had made from the capital, he said it had taken as much or more time to travel 'the last 20 or 30 miles' from Oxford to Banbury by road as it had 'the previous 100 miles' (sic) from London to Oxford by rail.

Everyone at the meeting accepted that the 'want of railway communication was obvious'. The only matter at issue was which company should provide it. After discussion, J.M. Severne, Esq., of Thenford House, proposed a resolution accepting the GWR plan as being the one which would be most advantageous to the town of Banbury, while Mr W. Bigg offered a counter-resolution. Further discussion then ensued but when put to the vote, the original motion was declared to have been carried unanimously 'amid vehement cheering', with 'not a hand being held up against it.'

This outcome was a little surprising, since there was a strong body of opinion in Banbury against the broad gauge and the *Banbury Guardian* carried articles in favour of the narrow gauge that summer. In fact, it appears that at least a quarter of those present at the meeting abstained from voting. Undaunted, Mr Saunders returned thanks for the confidence that the assembly had shown in the GWR scheme and promised 'to use every possible exertion to secure the Act, and to complete the works with all possible speed', pledging that the GWR would 'never be unmindful of the duty they owed to Banbury.'

Believing that they had local public opinion behind them, the GWR directors informed the company's August half-yearly meeting in London that, 'The necessity of the Oxford & Rugby line is universally admitted'. The shareholders were told that the university authorities had given their consent to the project and that meetings in Oxford and Banbury had passed unanimous resolutions in favour of it. Moreover, the principal landowners had been seen and there was every reason to count on their support. Thus the shareholders instructed the directors to apply to Parliament for permission to build the railway.

As required by law, the GWR made public its intention to apply for an Act of Parliament. In November, the local press published notices signed by the company's solicitors, who included Percival Walsh & Son in Oxford. The course of the line had already been determined by Brunel, the GWR engineer, who had completed his survey and collected information from his assistants, his aim being to find the easiest possible route. For instance, Heyford was surveyed to compare a route straight through the village with one winding round the valley – the latter course was chosen because it was much cheaper.

In planning the course of the line, Brunel seems to have experienced problems with some larger proprietors, who were traditionally reluctant to sell their land (often in the hope of increasing the compensation they would receive). For example, Lord Jersey, of Middleton Stoney, had to be placated with the promise that a station convenient for his use would be built at Somerton. Charles Cottrell Dormer, of Rousham, is reputed to have 'kicked the Surveyors' behinds' when they were surveying the Great Green at Heyford, but it is said he compensated them and offered no further resistance!

Books of Reference were prepared, containing maps and sections of the line along with the names of owners and occupiers of affected land, and were deposited with the clerks of places along the route by the end of 1844. In Oxford, one was lodged with the Clerk of the Peace at County Hall on 30 November. Places further afield got theirs a little later. William Wing records that it was not until 30 December that, 'Plans of a contemplated Railway, intended to pass through the parish of Steeple Aston, were deposited with the parish clerk, pursuant to the standing orders of the House of Commons'.

The notices referred to the GWR's plan for the construction and maintenance of a line, 'with all proper Works, Approaches, and Conveniences connected therewith'. It was to commence 'by a Junction with the Oxford branch' and terminate 'at or near Rugby'. In this way, the great British public learned of plans for the Oxford & Rugby Railway. However, because of the huge number of lines being proposed during this period of 'Railway Mania', Parliament decided that the Board of Trade should undertake a preliminary investigation of competing schemes, including the GWR and L&B plans for railways north of Oxford.

The inquiries were conducted by a committee of five board members who became known as the 'Five Kings'. They began their investigation in the autumn of 1844 and finally reported in January, 1845. In the event, their judgement – based purely upon 'commercial considerations' – went against the GWR's Oxford & Rugby Railway and was instead in favour of the L&B's alternative proposal. Their reasons included the 'undeniable evil of a break of gauge' and a desire to prevent the GWR from establishing 'a monopoly much more gigantic than that of the London & Birmingham'.

At local level too, the tide seemed to be turning against the GWR. Another important railway meeting was held at the Town Hall in Oxford on Friday 17 January 1845. This public meeting was convened by the Mayor, Mr Tarry, with both councillors and members of the public present. Robert Stephenson, engineer to the London & Birmingham Railway, was a prominent speaker and was able to sway the assembly in favour of his company's proposal. He claimed that the L&B scheme would give 'the greatest accommodation to the largest number of inhabitants'.

Robert Stephenson must have been preaching to the converted, as the majority of those present appear to have already embraced the L&B proposal. For instance, Councillor John Towle, who lived at Coldharbour, south of the city, was certainly no friend to the GWR, although he may well have had rather suspect motives. When the Oxford branch was under construction, he had delayed the building of a road-bridge (at Redbridge, on the Abingdon Turnpike) as the occupier of a piece of land there. He had hurriedly erected a 'house' of timber and brown paper, specifically to claim extra compensation from the GWR.

The councillor remarked on Oxford's unfavourable situation regarding the supply of coal, 'which was most important, to the poor especially'. Stephenson stated that his company would permit Derby coal to be delivered in Oxford at from 16s to 18s per ton, and Leicestershire coal at from 15s to 16s. Everyone knew what coal was worth at the pit head, he claimed, and the charge for transit on the

L&B 'would not exceed ld per ton per mile'. This response drew cheers from the assembly, which must have heartened Stephenson and his company.

The city's Postmaster, Mr Joseph Warne, spoke in a derogatory fashion about the standard of comfort and accommodation which the GWR afforded its second and third class passengers. He asked if the L&B railway 'was equally anxious to supply the hospitals and infirmaries with patients'. Stephenson replied that 'it was to the larger class – the poor and middle classes – that railways must look to for support, for they would never succeed while they worked for the rich only'. This populist sentiment again resulted in cheering.

At the end of the meeting, Mr Tarry denounced the GWR as 'the most rapacious of the monopolies that ever existed' and went on to move three resolutions saying firstly that the people of Oxford had not gained as much from railways as they might (a dig at the GWR), secondly that the proposed L&B line would benefit the city most, by giving Oxford a direct communication with the Midland coalfields and thus cheaper coal, along with a competing rail route to London, and thirdly that a memorial to this effect should be forwarded to the Board of Trade, 'praying that they will sanction the line'.

The resolutions were seconded by Mr Warne and were carried virtually unanimously by the meeting, with only one hand held up against, 'alone in its glory'. It was a complete reversal of the outcome at the meeting held in Oxford the previous summer. Coupled with the verdict of the 'Five Kings', the events of January 1845 must have tested the confidence of the directors of the GWR, whose Oxford & Rugby Railway scheme was now seriously threatened.

Nevertheless, the GWR and L&B companies duly submitted their respective schemes to Parliament. While the projects were being considered in London, they continued to excite opinion at local level in Oxford. The town's 'Railway Committee' reported to the full council at a meeting in the Town Hall on Thursday 10 April 1845. It recommended that the council withhold its support for the L&B line because 'other lines were in contemplation'. However, Councillor Towle protested against any further delay and moved that the committee's report 'be not adopted'.

Instead, Towle proposed that the council give its assent to the L&B scheme and this was seconded by Councillor Henry Haskins who gave notice that at the next council meeting he would move a petition in favour of the scheme, to be presented to Parliament. On the following Saturday, *Jackson's Oxford Journal* warned its readers that an alternative petition, in favour of the GWR's broad gauge scheme, 'is hawked about here on market days, with a view of getting a number of signatures to it, without reference as to what interest the parties have in the trade or prospects of this city'.

When the Council next met, on Tuesday 15 April, Haskins read his petition to the assembly, introducing it as, 'The humble petition of the Mayor, Aldermen, and Burgesses of the City and Borough of Oxford in Council assembled'. It stated that a railway from Oxford to the Midlands and beyond was regarded as an important objective by the council. Moreover, it was suggested that this objective would be secured with the greatest advantage 'by a Bill which is now before your Honourable House for making a Railway from the London & Birmingham Railway'.

The petition went on to argue in favour of a line constructed to the narrow gauge, for two main reasons. Firstly, to avoid the expense and inconvenience of a change of carriages for passengers or the reloading of goods and secondly, to reap the advantages of a readier connection with the coalfields of the Midland counties. In addition, it was claimed that the L&B line would afford a direct communication with a larger number of towns and a far greater population. Of course, there was a certain amount of exaggeration in these claims and most of the objectives could be equally well met by the GWR scheme.

Whatever the arguments for and against, Councillor Haskins got his way. 'Your petitioners therefore pray your Honourable House,' he concluded, 'that with all convenient speed the said Bill may pass into a law.' The petition was carried unanimously by the Council meeting and the seal of the City of Oxford was affixed to it before it was dispatched to Westminster. Parliament was advised in its deliberations by a committee comprising the 'Five Kings', who had already decided against the broad gauge. It looked as if the GWR had finally been defeated in the battle, and the L&B had won the day after all. But the war was not yet over.

# 3   In on the Act

As things turned out, the Oxford & Rugby line became the subject of a double irony. First, given the odds against it, the proposal should never have been sanctioned by Parliament. Second, in spite of gaining authorization, the line as planned was never actually built! Although it was a subsidiary company of the GWR, the Oxford & Rugby Railway had a nominal independence. As such, an attractive seal was prepared for it, on which the coats of arms of the two towns were interlinked and encircled by the name of the railway, along with the date 1845.

The Oxford & Rugby Railway Bill came before Parliament in the spring of 1845. It was paired with another GWR proposal, for an Oxford, Worcester & Wolverhampton Railway, and was opposed by the competing L&B narrow-gauge project, the London, Worcester & South Staffordshire Railway. In the House of Commons, the schemes passed their first and second readings, these being mere formalities anyway. The Oxford & Rugby Bill was read for a second time in the Commons on 10 March, but the debate that day is not recorded in *Hansard*, which was very selective at this period.

Away from Westminster, however, there was more scheming going on behind the scenes! Overtures were now made to the GWR by an independent concern, the Grand Junction Railway, which operated between Birmingham and the North-west. Keen to gain access to London independently of the L&B line, it sought the collaboration of the GWR in creating a new route to the capital. Its proposal was for a line from Birmingham to join the Oxford & Rugby Railway north of Banbury. In view of the precarious state of its own plans, the GWR was ready to listen.

Thus an agreement was drawn up 'for the formation of a Company to make a Railway from Birmingham to Oxford by Warwick to some favourable point on the Oxford & Rugby Railway near Fenny Compton, to be called – The Birmingham & Oxford Junction Railway'. The share capital of the new company was to be made up of £20 shares, the total divided evenly between the Grand Junction and Great Western railways. Each company appointed three of its own directors to a provisional board which was to control the affairs of the new concern.

Because the Grand Junction was built to the narrow gauge and the Great Western to the broad gauge, the question of gauge on the new line was to be 'left an entirely open one until the result of the Oxford & Rugby Bill be known'. However, mindful of its commercial interests, the GWR did insist that 'the London traffic to be brought over the said Birmingham & Oxford Junction Railway, is to be brought to the station at Oxford'. It was strictly forbidden for this traffic to be 'diverted or taken from the said Oxford Line or from the Great Western Line by any other railway'.

By the subscribers' agreement of 15 April, power was given to the provisional board to enter into contracts to sell or lease the undertaking to either the Grand Junction or Great Western railway if appropriate. 'Under no circumstances except defeat in Parliament shall this project be abandoned,' it was stated. If the Bill was defeated in Parliament, any alternative line to be applied for was to follow whatever route 'may then seem most advisable'. It was intended that the Bill should be applied for in the ensuing session of Parliament.

These stipulations were intended to secure the Birmingham & Oxford Junction Railway as an alternative to the L&B and to keep it out of the hands of the latter company. The line was soon supported by the merchants and manufacturers of the Birmingham district, who were unhappy with the L&B, which many of them believed was abusing its monopoly in the carriage of goods and charging extortionate rates. Perhaps for this reason, the L&B began to lose its advantage over the GWR, as the pendulum of railway politics swung in favour of the latter.

In Parliament, the Oxford & Rugby Railway Bill went on to receive detailed scrutiny at the committee stage. These proceedings lasted from 5 May to 4 June, and in those nineteen days 102 witnesses were heard who answered 12,148 questions. The witnesses included railway officials – among them the rival engineers Brunel and Stephenson – but most were industrialists, such as iron masters and colliery proprietors from the affected districts. All their evidence was recorded in a 700-page 'Blue Book', published by the Government.

Not entirely surprisingly, when the committee finally reported in early June it was in favour of the Oxford & Rugby and the Oxford, Worcester & Wolverhampton schemes of the GWR. However, in an attempt to alleviate the problem of the break of gauge, the committee's report contained a special clause requiring the GWR to add a third rail – to provide 'mixed gauge' track – on its Oxford & Rugby line if the Board of Trade asked it to. The L&B took its defeat very badly, and immediately set about drumming up opposition to parliamentary adoption of the report.

The L&B published notices to canvas support, in an attempt to have the report's decision reversed in Parliament. In response, the GWR's ally the Grand Junction Railway circulated a message to its shareholders on 11 June urging them to persuade any MPs they knew to attend a special meeting on 17 June. The directors of the Grand Junction Railway had resolved, through its shareholders, to solicit the aid of 'Members of Parliament in support of the Oxford & Rugby and the Oxford, Worcester & Wolverhampton projects'.

Their motives were spelled out in the circular. They felt that adoption of the narrow gauge scheme would add to the 'absolute monopoly' of the L&B south of Birmingham. 'Such extensive powers would be in the highest degree dangerous to the public, and inconsistent with the fair interests of the Grand Junction Company', it was suggested. In brief, they would be deprived of an alternative route to London if the L&B was allowed to build its narrow-gauge line, thus blocking competition in the shape of the GWR's broad-gauge line.

The report caused a stir at local level too, as is evidenced by an editorial published in *Jackson's Oxford Journal* in mid-June. 'Seldom, if ever, has any circumstance of a local kind excited so much interest as the decision of the Committee respecting the proposed Railways from Oxford to the North-Midland districts', it declared. It went on to say, 'The struggle has been called 'the Battle of the Gauges', and it has indeed been a fight, not between rival armies on the battlefield, but of contending capitalists fighting for territory'.

It went on to comment on the report's recommendation that mixed gauge be adopted at the behest of the Board of Trade. 'It is a strange and remarkable fact that the Committee have since shewn the most marked distrust of their own judgement: after having broken the communication from Oxford to the North, by adopting the scheme of the Great Western Company, the Committee have actually had a clause inserted in the Bill, binding the Company to lay down the narrow gauge five years hence, if required! – a most Irish procedure this.'

This last remark appears to have been a reference to the fact that two members of the committee were Irish. They had apparently supported the GWR scheme because Brunel had planned to continue the line on to Port Dynlleyn in Wales, where a new harbour was to built, providing a ferry link to Dublin. Whatever the truth of the matter, the newspaper contended that the inevitable break of gauge would do 'a great injury' to Oxford. Having 'done the mischief', the newspaper said of the committee, 'they patch it up, or try to patch it up, by this after-thought clause'.

The report came before the House of Commons on 20 June and was debated at some considerable length. Discussion of the Oxford & Rugby Bill was overshadowed by that of the Oxford, Worcester & Wolverhampton Bill, with which it was paired by the GWR. A record of the debate runs to two pages in *Hansard*. The fierce opposition inspired by the L&B was led by Richard Cobden, Member of Parliament and celebrated advocate of free trade. He proposed an amendment – possibly as a delaying tactic – asking for a Royal Commission to look into the gauge issue.

When the report on the Oxford & Rugby Bill was brought up, those MPs who opposed it moved 'that the consideration of the Report be further considered that day three months', so that the gauge issue could be dealt with separately. Mr W.R. Collett, seconding the amendment, argued that 'measures should be taken to have it ascertained whether the public at large would be most benefited by the broad or the narrow gauge'. It soon became evident that a large number of the Members present also wished to defer adoption of the report.

The chairman of the committee, Mr Shaw, explained that they had regarded the Oxford & Rugby Railway and the broad gauge as one and the same issue, and so wished both matters before the House 'to stand or fall together'. It was clear that a break of gauge must occur somewhere, and the question was 'whether the broad gauge was to go up to Rugby, or the narrow gauge to go down to Oxford'. Mr Home Drummond, speaking for the amendment, said that in his opinion Oxford was the proper place at which to make a change of gauge.

'The question before the House,' Mr Gisborne agreed, 'was whether the broad gauge was to extend much farther north than had been originally intended'. He considered Rugby a poor place to break the gauge, given its importance in the transport of coal: 'The greatest inconvenience would be felt if the coals were to be shifted to different wagons at Rugby, instead of being carried on without interruption to Oxford'. Mr Maclean spoke next, claiming that the cost of 'shifting the coals from one line to another would be enormous', increasing the price of 'coals for Oxford'.

There was a protest from Mr Newdegale, in support of the amendment, at 'having the broad gauge brought up to Rugby, to the serious injury of the manufacturers and millers of the north'. Mr Villiers Stuart, speaking against any postponement, believed that 'the bodies of trucks could easily be transshipped', and that he had seen it done successfully. Mr Ward disagreed, saying that he 'had no confidence in this alleged plan of transshipping the bodies of the trucks from lines of one gauge to those of a different gauge'. And so the debate proceeded to a division of the House.

The vote on the Oxford, Worcester & Wolverhampton Bill eclipsed that on the Oxford & Rugby Bill, although both were passed by majorities of about two to one. The former passed by 247 votes to 113, and the latter by 79 votes to 43. Cobden's amendment was lost, but only temporarily as he revived it a few days later and his resolution to establish a 'Gauge Commission' was adopted without opposition. It sat from August to December 1845 and the resulting Gauge Act (1846) ruled against any further broad-gauge lines being sanctioned.

The Great Western Railway's station at Oxford, *c*.1910. This station, on the Botley Road, was opened in 1852 when the GWR completed its main line through Oxford to Birmingham. (Courtesy of Kingfisher Postcards)

Nevertheless, the Oxford & Rugby Bill had safely passed its report stage in the House of Commons. It had its third reading there on 24 June, when there was another division, but no record of the debate is contained in *Hansard*. From here, it went on to the House of Lords, where their committee deliberated further. In spite of protracted opposition, unanimous support was forthcoming for the Bill, and it received the Royal Assent on 4 August 1845. At last, the GWR had acquired an Act authorizing construction of the Oxford & Rugby Railway for which it had fought so hard.

At a Special General Meeting held in Bristol on 14 August, the directors of the GWR were given authority to buy up the Oxford & Rugby Railway (along with two others, the Berks & Hants and Monmouth & Hereford railways). In return for defraying all their existing and future expenses, the 'rights, powers and privileges conferred upon those Companies by the respective Acts' would become the property of the GWR. The first (and only!) formal meeting of the Oxford & Rugby Railway Company was held at Paddington Station on 18 December, 'at one o' clock precisely', with six GWR directors in attendance to represent it.

Mr Henry Simonds was duly appointed chairman of the company's directors. It was noted that £600,000 capital had been subscribed according to a certificate, dated 13 December and signed by two Magistrates in the County of Oxford, Messrs J.W. Henley and W.H. Ashurst of Waterstock. At this meeting it was resolved to sell the Oxford & Rugby Railway to the GWR on the terms specified at the previous August meeting. (In the event, the Oxford & Rugby Railway became the Oxford & Rugby line of the GWR when the purchase was effected on 14 May 1846).

Initially, the GWR moved quickly and invited tenders for the work straight away. In the early days of railways, work on a line was often divided up among a number of contractors. By this date, it was more likely that just one firm would get a contract, although they might still appoint subcontractors for certain jobs. It was true that money could be made from railway contracting and many firms hoped for a quick profit, but many were ill-equipped to tackle the work they took on and they frequently over-stretched themselves; a lot of railway contractors went bankrupt.

The construction of the Oxford & Rugby line was let as a single contract in 1845. At a meeting of the company's General Committee on 11 September it had been reported that tenders had been received for 'the works on the Oxford & Rugby Line'. There is no indication in the minutes of the meeting as to what the main considerations might be in accepting a tender. Of course, it was important to drive a hard bargain, but (in view of the Birmingham & Oxford agreement) there was uncertainty about the line north of Banbury. However, two tenders were submitted to the meeting.

One was from Messrs Oldham, who offered to build the section of line from Banbury to Rugby in twenty-four months; the other was from Messrs B. & N. Sherwood, who offered to build the whole line within eighteen months. Messrs Sherwood, of Belvedere Place, Vauxhall Road, London, were supposedly contractors of 'experience and responsibility'. It was resolved that their tender be accepted, on condition that they undertake to finish the line from Oxford to Banbury in fifteen months, and the rest of the line on to Rugby in eighteen months, from the date of their occupying the land.

Subsequently, the GWR made more cautious progress with its Oxford & Rugby line. Messrs Sherwood moved 'on site' during the autumn and were keen to commence work, although they first required finance. They wrote to the GWR engineer, Brunel, asking for 'an advance of £10,000 on account of future Certificates for work to be done and on the security of the Plant now upon that line'. He raised the request at the General Committee Meeting on 1 January 1846 but it was refused on the grounds that the contract for the work was not yet 'drawn out and executed'.

Further into the New Year, on 12 March, Brunel reported to another meeting of the General Committee that he had arranged with Messrs Sherwood, 'as Contractors for the several separate Contracts on the Oxford & Rugby Line', the sums of money they should receive for each portion of the construction work. He added that he would report specifically on this matter at future meetings. This state of affairs does not give an impression of urgency on the part of the GWR to expedite the work – the official reason for the delay was that there was difficulty in getting possession of the land required.

However, there may have been other reasons. The outcome of the Birmingham & Oxford Junction scheme had itself been thrown into doubt around this time. The Grand Junction Railway had now defected to join the L&B, deserting their erstwhile GWR ally. Nevertheless, there were other parties still prepared to go ahead with the scheme, who lodged a Bill with Parliament for the session of 1846. In spite of violent opposition in the House of Lords, it received the Royal Assent on 3 August of that year as the Birmingham & Oxford Junction Railway Act.

The Act authorized the construction of a railway from Birmingham to a junction with the Oxford & Rugby line at Knightcote, about eleven miles north of Banbury, in the parish of Fenny Compton. It also offered the option of sale or purchase only to the GWR, the Grand Junction Railway no longer being so favoured. As things turned out, in 1848 the GWR did indeed secure control of the Birmingham & Oxford Junction Railway. Then, in 1849, the GWR abandoned the section of line from Fenny Compton to Rugby. So it was that the Oxford & Rugby Railway actually went from Oxford to Birmingham in the end!

# 4 Growing Pains

Even as late as the spring of 1846, construction of the Oxford & Rugby Railway had not been started, owing to the alleged delay in gaining possession of the land required. According to the GWR, this difficulty arose because of the insertion into the Act of a new clause relating to the payment of compensation for land purchase. It is generally true that if there was determined opposition to a new railway then landowners had to be bought off by the insertion of special clauses into an Act, or by especially favourable payments, before giving way to a railway company, although there is no evidence of such in this case.

In most cases, landowners stood to gain more than they lost with the coming of a railway. Indeed, the high cost of railways in Britain is partly a result of high claims for land and compensation. The acuteness shown by certain landowners in wringing money from railway companies often had to be seen to be believed. Some idea of what was involved may be gleaned from contemporary documents produced by the GWR to facilitate land purchase. For instance, documents exist relating to land purchase near Rugby at a place called Hillmorton, where the Oxford Canal Company operated a toll office.

A certain Edward Stafford was issued with notice of purchase on 27 July 1846. Signed by the GWR's Company Secretary, Charles Saunders, it referred to plots of land at Hillmorton, numbered 25 and 26 as identified in the Book of Reference lodged with the Clerk of the Peace for Warwickshire. The plots were 'required by the said Great Western Railway Company' which intended 'to take the same' by purchasing the land and 'all subsisting Leases, Terms, Estates and Interests therein', also paying compensation 'for any damage that may be sustained by you ... by reason of the execution of the works'.

The landowner was required to complete and return a 'Schedule of Claim' within twenty-one days, sending it either to the GWR's company offices at Paddington or to the company's solicitor, Charles Stevens, at 6, Frederick's Place, Old Jewry, London. This must have been done, as a 'Memorandum of Agreement' was signed on 24 September 1846 recording the purchase by the GWR. It was signed jointly by Richard Hall, 'an able practical Surveyor, nominated for and on behalf of the above Company', and Edward Stafford 'of Hill Morton, aforesaid, Yeoman', who agreed to accept £500 for his 2a. 0r. 30p. of land.

Of the total, £350 was for the land as such and £150 was compensation for severance and other damage. This was deemed to satisfy all claims for damage, loss or inconvenience, and 'for all culverts, bridges, drains, ways, passages, and watering places, either over or under the Railway of the said Company, or intercepted thereby'. The purchase soon proved unnecessary, however, and the land was not needed, as the Oxford & Rugby Railway never got to Hillmorton.

Moreover, the timing of the purchase seems odd, since it was in about August 1846 that the GWR directors 'decided to stop at Fenny Compton'.

The delay in starting construction of the line stimulated much criticism of the GWR from the inhabitants of places along its route. A letter from the Mayor of Banbury, Mr Richard Goffe, and other gentlemen was read to a meeting of the General Committee on 26 March 1846. It complained about the delay 'of the works on the Oxford & Rugby Railway' and asked what the intentions of the company were in this respect. The secretary had prepared a reply which was submitted to the meeting and approved. It was duly sent to the complainants in Banbury but appears to have done little to satisfy them.

A public meeting was next called in the town and held on 14 April, with the mayor in the chair and about 100 people present. The charge against the GWR was that up to the previous Wednesday (8 April) 'not a sod had been turned' on the line of the railway. Only the previous week, the contractors for the GWR had started work on the line, but in a very half-hearted fashion. Thus, in an opening speech, Colonel North was able to joke that '...the Oxford & Rugby Line is not yet commenced – I beg pardon, I understand there are two men and some posts and rails at Cropredy [laughter] – two men to commence a railway?'

The colonel was supported by the Revd Francis Litchfield, rector of Farthinghoe, who said that he had attended the railway meeting held in Banbury in 1844. On that occasion, Litchfield had supported the GWR scheme and claimed to have had the following conversation with Mr Frederick Barlow, a director: Litchfield – 'I hope you will justify by your acts what has been stated here today.' Barlow – 'Sir, I will pledge myself that, unless some unforeseen difficulties should arise, the force of which you will readily acknowledge, you shall ride in a train from Banbury to Oxford in twelve months from the passing of the Bill.'

If Barlow really had made such a rash promise, he and the other GWR directors must now have bitterly regretted it. A comparison was drawn between the Trent Valley and Oxford & Rugby lines, both authorized in 1845 and of about the same mileage. Construction of the former had commenced on 13 November 1845 with forty-eight miles of land purchased; construction of the latter had commenced on 9 April 1846 with 'not an acre paid for a month since'. The number of workmen employed in building the former line was 3,000; the number employed in building the latter line was deemed to be 'notten'.

In consequence, it was moved by Colonel North and seconded by the Revd G.M. Nelson that, 'The course pursued by the Great Western Railway Company, in so long deferring the commencement of the Line of Railway from Oxford to Rugby, and in now commencing, and with so small a force, in the Parish of Cropredy, on the Southam side of Banbury, is in direct violation of pledges given that no delay should take place, and that the line between Oxford and Banbury should be completed within a year from the date of their Act of Parliament.' There was a lot of support for this motion at the meeting.

However, there was some disagreement with this censure of the GWR. The local press commented that, 'respectable as it was, not half of those present took any part in the business of the meeting, and not one-third held up their hands in favour of any of the resolutions, while a very few opposed them'. Many of those present felt that in spite of the delay the GWR had now shown a determination to get on with the work. Nevertheless, at the end of the meeting a petition was organized, urging that the GWR should not receive Parliamentary Assent for any further railways until the Oxford & Rugby line was completed.

The petition was in fact raised and presented to the House of Commons although there was still strong support for the GWR in the town. At a General Committee meeting on 23 April an 'address of confidence' was presented by a Mr Moore of Banbury. Signed by many of the leading residents of the borough, it expressed their entire satisfaction with the Company and dissented from the views expressed in the petition. As construction work on the line had at last commenced, the GWR was less troubled in this respect – at least for a time – but further problems were about to arise, in respect of the 'gauge question'.

On 16 July 1846 the L&B Railway, with others, had been constituted as the London & North Western Railway. Within days of the creation of the LNWR the influence of Robert Stephenson, its engineer, seems to have been responsible for the resurrection of the gauge question. Thus, on 25 July, Captain O'Brien at the Board of Trade wrote to the GWR invoking the requirement that extra rails for narrow-gauge trains be laid on the broad-gauge Oxford & Rugby Line. On 3 August his letter was read to a General Committee meeting, at which the GWR's engineer, Brunel, was present to advise.

Brunel was instructed to consider the matter and report back. He was asked to provide the Board of Trade with detailed plans of an appropriate method for laying extra rails. Just to complicate things, in the autumn of 1846 the functions of the Board of Trade were taken over by the Railway Commissioners. On 23 November the commissioners' secretary, Frederick Bruce, wrote to the GWR again, asking for a description of the method they proposed to use to lay extra rails. At a General Committee meeting three days later the GWR directors replied to the effect that Brunel had not yet completed his report.

It was not until the New Year that the Railway Commissioners received Brunel's report. In it, he recommended 'mixed gauge' – that is, an additional third rail, with the outer rail of the three common to both broad- and narrow-gauge trains. The GWR directors invited the commissioners to Paddington on 25 February to see a model prepared by Brunel to demonstrate how mixed gauge worked. Afterwards, the directors took the commissioners to view newly laid mixed-gauge track in operation at Ealing, on the GWR main line.

The commissioners sent the report to Robert Stephenson at the LNWR for his comment. Six months later he sent in some lengthy 'Observations' strongly critical of the GWR engineer's mixed gauge proposal. Brunel responded angrily, rejecting Stephenson's observations and reminding the commissioners that they had actually seen mixed-gauge track in operation earlier in the year. They next consulted Captain Simmons of the Royal Engineers, who came down on the side of Brunel. Still uncertain of what to do, in November 1847 the Commissioners wrote to the GWR and proposed to defer any decision!

This was no good to the GWR, who replied that it was important that a decision should be reached soon. The Commissioners thereupon appointed Captain Simmons as Inspector-General of the railways and left him to take the decision. In a letter dated 2 March, 1848, he informed the GWR that he 'assented to the method proposed by Mr Brunel for laying the additional rails'. His decision was confirmed by Parliament as part and parcel of its consideration of the Bill for the purchase of the Birmingham & Oxford Junction Railway by the GWR, for which the ensuing Act supported Brunel's plan for third rail 'mixed gauge'.

In the meantime, serious delay had occurred with the construction work because the contractor had run into difficulties. At a General Committee meeting on 15 July 1847 Brunel reported on 'the progress of the works on the Oxford & Rugby Line and the very unsatisfactory state of the pecuniary affairs of the Contractors, Messrs B. and N. Sherwood'. The subject was discussed with the GWR solicitor, Mr Charles Stevens, on whose advice it was resolved that no further payments should be made to the contractor as it would be of no advantage to the company.

Arrangements were then made to take the work out of Messrs Sherwoods' hands. At a meeting on 5 August Brunel reported that he had 'taken the necessary steps to have the whole works measured up preparatory to a final settlement' being made. His plan to re-let the contract to 'more responsible parties' was approved by the directors. At another meeting on 28 October Mr Stevens reported that an agreement releasing Messrs Sherwood from their contract had been received from their solicitor, Mr Duncan. After discussion, detailed amendments were suggested but the release was accepted in principle.

The release was not fully concluded for a long time. In 1848 negotiations took place to purchase 'several Sheds containing tools and machinery belonging to Messrs B. & N. Sherwood on the Oxford & Rugby Line at Banbury'. The GWR agreed to pay £2,000 for the same, 'provided Mr Duncan undertook to distribute that sum to the parties who were Creditors in the Neighbourhood of the Works'. In 1849 arrangements were made with the trustees of Messrs Sherwood for the GWR to acquire rails 'now left in the possession of the Company for the Works on the Oxford & Rugby Line'.

Work on the line was suspended from the summer of 1847 until the spring of 1848, when new contractors began operations. These were Messrs I. & J. Tredwell, who already had the contract for building the GWR's Berks & Hants line on from Reading. At a General Committee meeting on 10 February 1848 an application from them was read out, requesting that their free travel pass from Paddington to Reading be extended on to Oxford, 'the transfer of their Plant and Materials from the Berks & Hants Line to the Oxford & Rugby Railway requiring their constant personal attendance between those places'.

Brunel reported that he was negotiating with Messrs Tredwell to complete the earthworks between Oxford and Banbury. An offer had also been submitted for the completion of the earthworks between Banbury and Fenny Compton by subcontractors. Following discussion, Brunel was instructed to make arrangements with a view to restarting the construction work on the Oxford & Rugby line. In April 1848 the new contractors began work, but for financial reasons they were ordered to proceed slowly and to confine themselves mainly to essential work, such as culverts, river crossings and public roads.

Progress remained very limited for a whole year, but the GWR engineer then seems to have become impatient to have the job expedited more quickly. A letter from Brunel was read to a General Committee meeting on 5 April 1849; in it he urged that the work 'should be proceeded with more vigorously during the ensuing summer', and was concerned that it should be completed before the onset of the winter flooding. He recommended the expenditure of £7,000 per month for the next five or six months and specified certain land which 'should now be agreed for and possession taken'.

Some idea of the cost of land purchased by the GWR for the Oxford & Rugby line can be gleaned from the official Cash Book of the company, which records payments made throughout this period – that is, from 1846 to 1849. The railway crossed the Oxford Canal in many places and as a result the Canal Company received the considerable sum of £32,326 18s to cover compensation, purchase of land and the public house at Aynho. Various payments were made to Oxford colleges, including Corpus Christi, Exeter, Lincoln and Merton, with St John's College receiving the largest sum at £2,600.

Among individual landowners, the Duke of Marlborough seems to have been paid the most, receiving £5,000 from the GWR in September 1846, for instance. Other titled individuals who received substantial payments were Lord Abingdon (£1,900 in 1848), Lord Valentia (£1,500 in 1846), Sir Trevor Wheeler (£1,900 in 1847) and Sir George Dashwood (£2,055 in 1846). As well as payment for land, the latter received £41 in 1849 'in respect of his manorial rights in Tackley Common'. The Tackley commoners themselves received payment of £786 for land on the common which was taken for the railway.

There were numerous other payments, both large and small. In 1846, the Oxford Freemen received £1,248 for land at Port Meadow, while in 1849 the Banbury Race Committee was paid £50 compensation for damage to its race course. Various parishes along the route received contributions to their rates. For example, in 1846 poor rate contributions of a pound or so were made to the parishes of Neithrop, Cropredy and Aynho, and in 1848 to Middleton Cheney, Somerton and Heyford. In 1849 the Surveyors of Highways at Cropredy were paid £125 'for damage done to parish roads'.

Land purchases were made primarily with a view to completing the section of line from Oxford to Banbury as soon as possible and the continuation of it from Banbury on to Fenny Compton 'at the time needful for the opening of the Birmingham & Oxford Railway', which would connect with it there. By now, it had definitely been decided to scrap the section between Fenny Compton and Rugby. The state of this section, it was announced at a General Committee

Knightcote 'junction', near Fenny Compton (looking North). The junction was never built. The main line from Oxford curves away to the left. The embankment curving away to the right runs for a quarter of a mile but never carried track, as the line to Rugby was never built.

meeting on 18 October 1849, was that of 'all purchases being stopped and no work commenced ... having regard to the final abandonment of it'.

At the point of the junction of the Oxford & Rugby line with the Birmingham & Oxford line at Knightcote, near Fenny Compton, about a quarter of a mile of embankment had been thrown up in the direction of Rugby but it was never used. The earthworks which were actually utilized amounted to over thirty-five miles. Payment to Messrs Tredwell, for completing the earthworks on the section from Oxford to Banbury, amounted to £85,000. As of the autumn of 1849, the total costs of the line were £760,000 for the Oxford-Banbury section and a further £227,000 for the Banbury-Fenny Compton section.

In bringing the project to this point, it has to be said that the GWR was not the only company to experience problems at this time. The 'Railway Mania' was over now and railway building was beset by financial crises and protracted delays. Both share prices and dividends fell by half between 1846 and 1849. Total authorized mileage fell from a peak of over 4,500 miles in 1846 to 1,300 in 1847, then 300 in 1848 and a mere seventeen miles in 1849. Many of the lines started in the late 1840s were only completed in the face of great difficulty. In this respect, the Oxford & Rugby line was by no means unique.

# 5 Men at work

The construction of a railway required the joint efforts of a large number of men. Long before any building work was done, it was the task of the railway engineer and his assistants to devise the best route for the projected line. In the case of the Oxford & Rugby line, the GWR had matters well in hand from the outset. Even before the first train arrived in Oxford, surveys were underway in the Banbury region. 'The surveying of the district is still going on,' it was reported on 30 May 1844, 'several engineers having been actively employed for several days past'. The GWR engineer, Isambard Kingdom Brunel, had overall responsibility for surveying the terrain between Oxford and Rugby, although in reality his assistant, T.H. Bertram, oversaw most of the actual construction work on the new line from Oxford to the Midlands.

The Cherwell Valley offered the railway a relatively easy-going course on its way north from Oxford to Rugby, but while the river meandered lazily through its incised and twisting valley, the railway had to find a more straightforward course. Thus, the latter necessitated the building of embankments across the open lowlands – which were liable to flooding – and the digging of cuttings through the spurs of higher ground. There was work enough to be done in the softer clay earth but in the harder soils there were rocky outcrops to be blasted through – a rather different proposition. Frequent flooding, to which the Cherwell Valley had always been prone, even in summer, became more common as a result of railway building.

In 'this alluvial territory', said the contemporary local historian William Wing, the disturbance to natural drainage caused by the construction of the railway interrupted the free flow of water into the River Cherwell, increasing the risk of flooding. Just as in earlier years the river had been diverted so that the canal could occupy its course near Heyford, it was now redirected yet again so that the railway line might occupy the riverbed this time. Otherwise, the chief culprits were the high embankments between Kidlington and Somerton, with associated culverts and channels. Although numerous small underbridges had to be constructed across the canal, with sufficient headroom for canal craft to pass beneath, it was recognized that, all in all, the engineering work involved was 'not of a heavy character'.

The physical labour in railway construction, as in canal building, was supplied by 'navigators', or 'navvies' as they were more usually known. Navvy labourers were paid two or three times as much as agricultural labourers, and this is what induced men to leave the land for railway construction. Some came from Ireland and Scotland, others from the farms of England itself. The navvies truly earned their money, literally risking life and limb to construct the permanent way on which the trains were to run. Using only picks and shovels, they filled horse-drawn wagons with tons of 'muck' (earth and rock) every day. It was their sheer muscle power that built the embankments, cuttings, bridges and other civil engineering works. By May 1848 there were 188,000 navvies building 3,000 miles of railway lines across the country.

For their labours, the navvies were paid according to the tasks they undertook – and the prevailing economic circumstances! Wages were highest in the boom years, but dropped by a third in the slump years. In 1846, skilled men such as bricklayers, carpenters and blacksmiths were paid 30s per week, and masons 33s (but by 1851, the weekly rate for all of them was only 21s). For unskilled men like pickmen and shovellers, weekly rates were 24s and 22s 6d respectively in 1846 (and only 15s and 14s in 1851). In 1846, the regular navvies earned 4s a day and even farm labourers new to the job could earn 2s 6d a day. Local landowners had various reasons to fear the onset of railway construction, and early in 1846 Sir Thomas Cartwright, Squire of Aynho, wrote nervously to Samuel Field, his land agent, worrying about the navvies' arrival.

Following the appointment by the GWR of Messrs Sherwood as contractors for the Oxford & Rugby Railway in the spring of 1846, the first railway navvies appeared in the Cherwell Valley. When they descended on previously quiet and peaceful communities they had an effect on the local people out of all proportion

OXFORD IN THE FUTURE, OR THE NEW FRESHMAN

Navvy: 'Gallon o' audit ale, Guv'nor, please. I's got t' blunt to pay vor'n.

Some contemporary critics were concerned about the impact of trailway workers on the local community. This cartoon appeared in *Punch* on 9 September 1865, after the GWR decided to establish a carriage and wagon works at Oxford.

to their numbers. The 150 railway navvies and their families imported into Cassington to build the southern section of the Oxford & Rugby line apparently demoralized the resident agricultural labourers, and in such a small place the five public houses opened to cater for the navvies had a bad effect on the farmworkers. Antagonism might arise between navvies and villagers, although for every instance of enmity there were others indicative of friendliness, at least as far as the Cherwell Valley is concerned.

Construction of the Oxford & Rugby line actually started on the northern section. After a long delay, *Jackson's Oxford Journal* reported that the first sod of earth was cut – without ceremony – on Wednesday 8 April 1846, in a meadow in the occupation of Mr William Anker at Cropredy. By mid-April there were fifty men at work here, and there was much activity at Fenny Compton where '70 labourers are at work, large brick kilns are in the course of erection, and a great quantity of materials are collected for the construction of the line'. The GWR, it was said, 'notwithstanding the unforseen difficulties which have arisen since their commencement', should be praised for displaying 'a determination which proves that the Company are desirous of redeeming as far as is possible the time hitherto lost'.

As each week passed more land was purchased, new materials arrived on site and fresh men continued to be engaged, so that 'the work begins to display itself to the public eye'. A special ceremony was held in Mr Anker's field at Cropredy on Thursday 30 April, when the first brick for a bridge under the railway was laid 'in a scientific manner'. Performed by the company's engineer, Mr James, the ceremony was watched by the company's agents, Mr Gooch and Mr Purnell, along with a crowd of spectators. Afterwards 'success was drank (sic) to the undertaking' and three cheers were given for the broad gauge. In May, 1846, construction began at three points near Banbury, and on Monday 1 June workmen began to demolish a terrace of houses, known locally as Waterloo Place, which had for years been 'an intolerable nuisance'.

Waterloo had been built earlier in the nineteenth century on the Northamptonshire side of Banbury bridge, and quickly gained a reputation as a notorious source of moral infection. In the 1830s it harboured pickpockets and was blamed for a series of robberies. At a court case in 1844 it was revealed that lodging houses here, kept by Thomas Ward, accommodated criminals visiting Banbury races. The Northamptonshire gentry considered buying and demolishing Waterloo but the GWR did this for them in 1846, thus ridding the town of a resort of vagrants and thieves. (There was a scare in January 1849, when railway workmen dug up a male skeleton near the south wall of Banbury bridge. Iinitial fears were that it might be a victim of the inhabitants of Waterloo, but tests showed later that this was unlikely to be so.)

In the summer of 1846, the railway at Banbury bridge was progressing well. South of the existing road, a new and 'massive, substantial, extensive arch' had been erected, crossing both the River Cherwell and the line. The projected line was fenced out from Banbury in the direction of Kings Sutton, with gangs of labourers 'busily engaged digging and levelling the earth, laying down sleepers, etc.' The line was now progressing rapidly at Cropredy and Hardwick, while navvies were also employed at Fenny Compton, Grimsbury, Aynho, Heyford and Steeple Aston. The inhabitants of the town watched in fascination as the construction work went ahead and expected – so it was reported – 'to be allowed to travel to Oxford and London by railway in a few months'. This was a rather optimistic hope by any stretch of the imagination.

A special arrangement was made with the contractors to keep clear of the ground used for Banbury racecourse until after the event, which was held on Tuesday 4 August 1846. In return for this consideration, the 'most prominent point of attraction' at the racecourse was a stand erected by the GWR for the convenience of themselves and friends. Sadly, the day was spoiled by very wet and rainy weather. Indeed, there were long spells of inclement weather in this period, so that the cold and wet began to slow down work on the line. The economic climate also took a turn for the worse and it was within a year of the race that B. and N. Sherwood found themselves in financial trouble, bringing construction of the railway to a halt. With little to do, the underemployed navvies played a boisterous part in the Banbury election of July 1847.

In the autumn of 1847 it was reported that the Oxford & Rugby line 'presented a melancholy aspect of desolation'. So matters stood until April 1848, when there was 'a delay attendant on the line forming from Oxford to Rugby, which still remains in a dormant state'. However, it was at about this time that the GWR installed Messrs Tredwell as contractors for the railway and construction was resumed. By June, the works had been 're-commenced with vigour', gangs of men being employed both day and night at several places on the line. In July, *Jackson's Oxford Journal* said that it could see 'no reason why the Great Western Railway Company should not allow a trip to Banbury on the Oxford & Rugby Line before Christmas'. Even at this stage, such speculation was still a trifle optimistic to say the least.

The summer of 1848 witnessed a nasty incident of navvy misbehaviour at Banbury. On the evening of Saturday 24 June, near to the bridge, a subcontractor, Mr Henry Whiteman, was paying his men when – for reasons which are not apparent – some of them attacked him. He had paid about half the men before 'he was suddenly and violently assaulted by a number of navvies, whose intention was to have swept off the whole of the cash then lying on the table, amounting to nearly £120'. Four of the ringleaders knocked Whiteman to the ground and kicked him 'in the most brutal manner' before drawing knives and attempting to stab him. In spite of the alleged severity of the attack, Whiteman managed, 'from some unexplained circumstance,' to escape from his attackers after losing only about £19.

The navvies pursued Whiteman to his house, and his life was only saved by the intervention of a neighbour, the Revd Thomas Mardon. He fled again, to the nearby toll house, but by now the alarm had been raised and the authorities were soon on the scene. Arrests took place, so that 'before twelve o'clock seven

High Street, Kings Sutton, *c.*1920. It was at Kings Sutton ('Twyford') that Robert Beckingham was injured by a wagon in1848. (Courtesy of Kingfisher Postcards)

of the ringleaders were in Banbury gaol; three have since been apprehended, and are now remanded until Saturday morning'. The navvies included some from surrounding villages as well as from more distant parts of the country. A week later Whiteman was reported to be 'recovering from the wounds inflicted upon him', while the navvies responsible for his injuries had been committed to Northamptonshire Assizes where, no doubt, they were dealt with accordingly.

Construction was in full swing at this time and the navvies seem to have been working under some pressure, as a result of which accidents occurred. On 25 August a navvy identified simply as 'one of Mr J. Plowman's labourers' was hurt at 'Gibraltar' (Bletchingdon). He was driving a team of horses with a load of stones 'when some fell on him and broke his leg'. On 1 September another navvy, named Robert Beckingham, was injured at 'Twyford' (Kings Sutton). He 'slipped down' while working and a wagon ran over his leg, 'causing serious injuries', but it was reported that he was progressing favourably.

On other occasions, the outcome of workaday mishaps was far more serious, with fatalities resulting either directly or indirectly from accidents to the navvies of the Oxford & Rugby line. A navvy named Henry Wakeford, of Petworth in Sussex, died in August 1848 from an illness thought to have been brought on 'by his falling into the Cherwell when engaged at his labour' as a carpenter. He had been taken to the Infirmary at Oxford but subsequently died. Having lodged at Kidlington prior to his illness, he was buried in the churchyard there. 'The deceased was followed to his grave by 25 of his fellow labourers from the railway works,' it was reported. In November 1851 another navvy, named John Pilcher, was injured when he fell at work and a ballast truck ran over his arm, which was 'much fractured'. He too was taken to the Infirmary in Oxford but died a few days later. He was buried beside Wakeford in the churchyard at Kidlington, his funeral procession being followed by sixty of his fellow workmen and 150 villagers.

By the summer of 1848 newspaper reports showed that construction work on the line was proceeding rapidly. In July the new bridge at Banbury – typical of the more expensive work – was well in hand. In August work was restarted at Steeple Aston by 'blasting the rocks and laying in of roads'. In September, at 'Gibraltar' near Bletchingdon, a number of masons were employed in erecting a stone bridge to carry the turnpike road across the railway. At Langford Lane near Kidlington, a new railway bridge was almost finished and it was planned to build another over the canal here, replacing an existing narrow structure. Clearly, the work had found a new impetus but it was not enough to satisfy all the GWR's critics, and it was obvious that the faith of the local newspaper's correspondents was not shared by everyone. At the annual Root Show, held in Heyford Market Place on Monday 25 September 1848, a Mr Wyatt said during the award ceremony that he was surprised that among the competitors for prizes that day he did not see the directors of the Oxford & Rugby Railway. To laughter, he joked that 'they had plenty of deep soil wherein to grow long mangold wurzel, and plenty of time, apparently, to end several crops before their line would be fit for traffic.'

The weather created more serious problems for the GWR on Sunday 1 October, when the district experienced the highest floods known for many years. The water rose rapidly and did a lot of damage to bridges and culverts along the line. A pile-driving machine was washed down and a number of barrows and planks were carried away by the floodwaters.

Nevertheless, as 1848 drew to a close the state of the line showed visible progress. At Langford Lane, the railway bridge was complete and the canal bridge was 'widened and materially improved for traffic'. The line was ballasted between here and 'Gibraltar', where the bridge carrying the turnpike was open to traffic and the cutting about three-quarters finished. The works were 'in a forward state' at Tackley and from here to Banbury workmen were still occupied. However, at Heyford construction was proceeding more slowly, and there were 'only about 40 men on the line near this place'. Early in the new year it was reported that 'of late a number of workmen have been discharged', and the works were 'now in a state of slow progression', which was in keeping with the policy adopted by the GWR directors.

The rundown in employment may help to explain an incident which took place in the spring of 1849, involving Charles Belcher of Tackley, 'a ganger on the Oxford & Rugby Railway'. Belcher was caught one night on the estate of C.C. Dormer, Esq., at Rousham (Heyford), 'with a gun and a dog', being apprehended by a gamekeeper named Allen. The poacher's dog was shot dead on the spot by

A flood at Botley Road railway bridge in Oxford, *c*.1965. The area adjacent to the railway through Oxfordshire has always been prone to flooding. (Courtesy of R.H.G. Simpson)

the gamekeeper. Belcher found himself before the bench at the Deddington Petty Sessions on 10 March 1849, where he was convicted of poaching and fined £3. Interestingly, at the next County Court, Belcher brought an action against Allen in an attempt to recover £10, 'the amount of a dog which defendant shot on the high road'. He was only awarded £3 in total, for compensation and costs, but at least he recovered the sum he had been fined!

In the spring of 1849, *Jackson's Oxford Journal* gave a resumé of progress to date on the Oxford & Rugby line. It said that 'the rate of progress has been very limited during the winter'. On the southern section, about ten miles of line – from Wolvercote to Tackley – were ballasted and ready for rails to be laid, with another seven miles towards Banbury ready to be ballasted. On the northern section, about five miles of line beyond Banbury were partially ballasted, with another two miles of earthwork completed as far as Claydon. The cutting at Fenny Compton and the embankments as far as the junction at Knightcote were 'in progress'. However, nothing had been done between here and Rugby except for the quarter of a mile of embankment – destined never to be utilized by the railway that was eventually built.

In the summer of 1849, the *Banbury Guardian* reported on the dramatic pyrotechnics in the rocky outcrops north of Cropredy, through which the navvies had to blast a cutting for the railway. Many local people gathered to watch and the

The River Cherwell passes under Cropredy Bridge, the site of a Civil War battle in 1644. At this point the river flows southwards to its confluence with the Thames at Oxford.

newspaper drew a parallel with another historic event – the Civil War battle at Cropredy bridge in 1644. It was pleased to reflect that 'on the very spot where two centuries earlier the conflicting armies of the Royalists and the Parliamentarians were engaged in mortal combat, a troup of men were now engaged in using gunpowder for a far different and much nobler object'. This objective, the newspaper went on to explain, was 'that of promoting a spread of commerce and speedy transit between the metropolis of England and the metropolis of the north'.

Everything on the southern section was in a more advanced state by the summer of 1849. On two-thirds of the line the ballasting was 'complete and ready to receive the permanent way'. From Banbury to the outskirts of Oxford the works at the bridges were virtually complete. It was in the vicinity of the city that the bulk of the works to complete the railway had yet to be done, and these were 'being proceeded with rapidly'. At the end of June, a large number of workmen were now employed here and 'active preparations have been made towards the formation of the Oxford portion of this line'. By this date, too, the directors of the GWR had decided on an interim goal for their Oxford & Rugby line, the opening of a single line only from Oxford to Banbury just as soon as this aim could be realized.

# 6   Open for business

The GWR, victor in 1845, now had good reason to seek a rapid push on Banbury. The LNWR, its arch-rival, had not admitted defeat or surrendered. On the contrary, the latter company had launched a counterattack on the region, and the speed of its approach suggested that it would overtake the supposed winner. As the GWR's Oxford & Rugby Railway was being built, the opposition's own project had been advancing on its flanks in the guise of the LNWR's Buckinghamshire Railway. This was a modified version of their original scheme, and comprised a line from Bletchley (on the LNWR trunk route) to Verney Junction, from which it forked north-west to Banbury and south-west to Oxford in a two-pronged attack.

As the threat began to materialize, the GWR directors realized that the faltering progress of its Oxford & Rugby line was inadequate, and that something had to be done to secure the territory for themselves. Thus they decided to open a single line from Oxford to Banbury in the first instance. The decision was finalized at a General Committee meeting on 12 July 1849. The reason for doing so was spelled out explicitly at the meeting – it was 'in order to prevent the traffic which now comes to the Oxford Station being abstracted by the Buckinghamshire Line being finished to Banbury as intended by the London & North-Western Company, who propose opening it in March, 1850'. Speed was of the essence.

Previously, the GWR engineer, Brunel, had been instructed to prepare a statement of 'the probable amount of Traffic and an Estimate of the actual cost in working the Line between Oxford and Banbury with four daily Trains'. He gave a verbal report which was discussed at this meeting. He calculated that the sum of £110,000 was still required to complete the railway to Banbury as a single line. This included the use of the 'present station at Oxford' and a new station at Banbury, along with other intermediate stations. Of the total, up to £75,000 would be due to the contractor (Messrs Tredwell) to complete the works on the line. The rails and timber for the track were 'already provided and paid for'.

Having considered the matter, the directors were satisfied that it would be advantageous to bring into use the Oxford-Banbury section 'to maintain that Traffic which now comes from the District to Oxford'. Accordingly, it was resolved that 'the Works between Oxford and Banbury be proceeded with so as to complete a single line of Broad Gauge Rails from the present Oxford Station to Banbury to be opened for Public Traffic early in next spring – as recommended by the Engineer'. Brunel was further instructed to produce a written report of his estimates, which was read to a General Committee meeting on 26 July, with a brief 'Report of the GWR Engineer' being published in the local press in late August 1849.

Heyford Station, looking south, *c.*1910. This station opened in 1852, when it was one of only three intermediate stations between Oxford and Banbury. (Courtesy of Kingfisher Postcards)

So the GWR's push on Banbury began in earnest. By the spring of 1850, little remained to be done except building the stations and laying the tracks – the 'permanent way' – upon which the trains would run. For example, at Banbury 'there appears to be little to be done now but laying down the sleepers and rails and erecting the station', it was reported in February. Over the next few months, the intermediate stations were in the course of construction at 'Woodstock' (Bletchingdon), Heyford and Aynho. As late as 18 July, the GWR purchased '1 acre of extra land' from Corpus Christi college as the site for Heyford station, paying £300 for the land and as compensation 'in lieu of 4 bridges'.

However, the laying of the track proved less straightforward. The contract for this work had been given to the firm of George Hennet, who had been providing ballast, timber and rails for the Oxford & Rugby line since 1846. Much of the ballast had been dug from fields at Hinksey (leaving a large lake afterwards), most of the timber had been imported through the Merchant Venturers' premises at Bristol and the rails were made in Wales and Staffordshire by ironmasters like William Crawshay, Arthur Hill and Guest Lewis & Co. Between 1846 and 1852, when the line was completed throughout, George Hennet's were paid a total of over two-and-a-half million pounds for supplying and laying the track.

The laying of the permanent way was a problem because it resurrected the gauge question. Pressured by Hennet's for guidance, Brunel sought the advice of the GWR directors at a General Committee meeting on 7 March 1850. The directors confirmed their desire for a single broad-gauge line from Oxford to Banbury, 'so as to dispense with any Mixed Narrow Gauge until the whole of the line (to Birmingham) shall be completed'. Brunel was told to correspond with the Railway Inspector, Captain Simmons, about the matter and on 4 April Brunel informed the directors of Simmons' reply. The matter was to be taken up formally with the Railway Commissioners – who had already insisted on mixed gauge!

In April, therefore, Charles Saunders, GWR secretary, wrote a letter to the Railway Commissioners asking them to allow the railway to open as a broad-gauge line only as far as Banbury. The commissioners sent a copy of the letter to the Buckinghamshire Railway Company for its comment but vacillated over their own verdict. Captain Simmons was more decisive and said that he could see no reason to object to the GWR's request, since the Oxford & Rugby line had no connection with any narrow-gauge lines as yet. He did not consider the interests of the public would be 'injuriously affected by its opening on the Broad Gauge only', provided the line became mixed gauge when extended northwards.

The Buckinghamshire Railway and its parent company, the LNWR, played for time, as well they might since their own line was nearing completion. Given that Oxford was already served by a railway, this section was deemed less urgent. However, the section to Banbury was judged to be potentially more lucrative and this became a priority. A site for a station had been found at Merton Street in Banbury in 1849. The LNWR line received its Government inspection in April 1850 and the first public passenger trains arrived in Banbury on 1 May, ahead of the GWR. To celebrate the occasion, the neighbourhood of the station took on the appearance of a fairground, with flags, booths, stalls and a brass band.

Meanwhile, the GWR had grown impatient with the Railway Commissioners and pressed ahead regardless. By the summer, the single broad-gauge line was finished and the directors invited Captain Simmons to inspect it on 27 August. In his report he wrote that, 'The works are not of a heavy character'. He commented specifically on the three-arched, wrought-iron bridge over the River Thames at Oxford, but was more perfunctory in his treatment of all the other timber-framed, cast-iron bridges. 'They appear to be of ample dimensions and strength to perform the duties required of them,' he stated. The track was typically broad-gauge in style, of 'bridge' rails laid upon longitudinal wooden sleepers.

The GWR line from Oxford to Banbury was opened on Monday 2 September 1850. Initially, trains left from the existing terminus station near Folly Bridge. They then had to make an inconvenient manoeuvre, reversing at Millstream Junction (Hinksey), before heading north. The new railway was, for the time being, merely a twenty-four-mile-long rural branch line with three intermediate stations, at 'Woodstock' (Bletchingdon), Heyford and Aynho (later known as

'Aynho for Deddington'), which originally seem to have comprised prefabricated timber buildings. The new GWR station at Banbury was a wooden construction with an overall roof, designed by R.C. Pauling and built to the contemporary Brunel style.

All the works were completed for a double line, even though only one broad-gauge line had been laid, on the 'down' (western) side of the track bed. A report on the opening of the railway in *Jackson's Oxford Journal* commented that the new line 'appears to have been remarkably well constructed, and runs through a district pleasingly diversified with wood, hill and dale'. The Cherwell Valley did indeed provide a pleasantly scenic route, with both the river and the canal to keep the railway company for much of the way. 'There was no public demonstration' on the opening day, 'and the number of persons along the line, attracted by curiosity, were but few', according to the press reports of the day.

The inaugural service consisted of four trains each way each day, all of them worked by 'one engine in steam', (the normal branch line practice), with the same driver regularly in charge of the locomotive. This man was George Thompson, who drove the train from Oxford to Banbury day-in-day-out until he was killed in an accident on the line just over two years later. First and second class single fares from Oxford to Banbury were 4s 6d and 2s 6d respectively, with return fares at a reduction of a quarter on the double fares. London was now only two and a half hours from Banbury, the respective first and second class single fares to Paddington being 17s 6d and 14s 6d (express) and 16s and 11s (ordinary train).

In the first week of operation, it was reported that trains on the Oxford-Banbury line were carrying 'as fair an allowance of passengers as could have been expected'. Patronage of the line was somewhat discouraged by the inaugural timetable, as the first train departed from Oxford at 10.05, and the last train returned from Banbury at 16.05. The opening day coincided with Feast Monday at Heyford, where David Kirby, 'sawyer' of Upper Heyford, bought the first ticket issued at the station. On Banbury market day (Thursday), 'the trains conveyed a much larger number of passengers than on any previous day'. Many of them were farmers and dealers with business to transact in the market houses during the day.

Awaiting the first train from Oxford, the Banbury station presented a busy scene, 'in consequence of the throng of persons congregated there to witness the arrival of the train bringing friends who were wont to come by road'. Later, in the market houses, people expressed a unanimous feeling of 'disappointment and dissatisfaction' about the limited time the trains allowed them in Banbury, but it was hoped that this inconvenience was only temporary – due to the line being opened at short notice – and that it 'will be speedily obviated'. There was a general willingness to support the new line provided 'a liberal spirit, and a desire to accommodate the public, are evinced by the Great Western Company'.

The GWR was soon displaying such a spirit, with regard to both its normal and special train services. Three weeks after the opening, on Monday 23 September,

The approach to Oxford Station (down side) around 1950. The buildings seen here date from the Victorian rebuild of the station in 1891. (Courtesy of Kingfisher Postcards)

an excursion was put on from Banbury to London, 'at the low charges of 7/6 and 4/6' (first and second class return fares). Sadly, not every member of the public showed the same spirit. In the spring of 1851 the local press carried stories that on several occasions passengers travelling in trains on the Banbury branch 'have been greatly annoyed, and in some instances injured, by the wanton conduct of boys and others throwing stones at the train as it passed'. Apparently, this antisocial behaviour took place mainly in the Deddington area.

Even as the branch trains were running, work was going on to finish the line according to plan, that is as a double line from Oxford to Birmingham. In the summer of 1851 the GWR was completing the new public road bridge over the River Cherwell at Banbury, prior to opening the northward extension of the line, 'which is rapidly progressing'. By the end of the year it was reported that the route was 'occupied by a great number of workmen' and – with the usual optimism – 'we hope to have the pleasure to announce, in a few months, that the line from Oxford to Banbury and Leamington (if not to Birmingham) will be completed'. In fact, completion was still nearly a year away at this time.

At the southern end of the line, a new Oxford station was under construction at Botley Road, on the west side of the town, close to where the LNWR had already opened its own terminus at Rewley Road on 20 May 1851. (The Buckinghamshire Railway had been extended from Verney Junction to Islip on 1 October, and thence to a station at Stratfield Brake, on the Oxford-Banbury Road, by 2 December 1850). Between Oxford and Banbury the GWR had laid a second set of rails, of mixed gauge, on the 'up' (eastern) side of the track bed, although they were not yet in use. The section from Banbury to Knightcote Junction was finished and the permanent way was being laid early in 1852.

At the northern end of the line, the Birmingham & Oxford Junction Railway was being built by the celebrated contractors Messrs Peto & Betts. Work on this line had started in 1847 but was dogged by financial problems for two years. From 1849 things moved more quickly, although the construction of a station at Snow Hill in Birmingham was not begun until January 1852, owing to difficulties in obtaining possession of the properties to be cleared from the site. This railway was also laid to the mixed gauge. At long last, after being inspected twice by the Board of Trade in September 1852 the new main line from Oxford to Birmingham was given official approval to open throughout the whole of its length.

The day chosen for the commencement of public passenger services was 1 October 1852 but on the day before, a special excursion along the line was arranged for GWR directors, officers and friends. The special train, of ten carriages, was hauled by the *Lord of the Isles*, a new locomotive which had recently been displayed at the Great Exhibition. The special left Paddington at 09.00 and was due in Oxford at 10.15, but ran late owing to delays *en route*. Meanwhile, at Oxford, the 09.55 stopping train to Banbury was being held back to give the special a clear run through. However, after holding it for about twenty-five minutes, the railway authorities let it go on its way as the excursion was behind time.

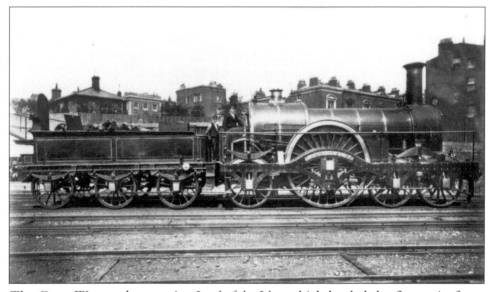

The Great Western locomotive *Lord of the Isles*, which hauled the first train from Oxford to Banbury in 1852. It was damaged in the crash at Aynho but was later repaired and put back into service. (Courtesy of Kingfisher Postcards)

Aynho Station, *c*.1920. This station was another of the original three stations between Oxford and Banbury, dating from 1852. (Courtesy of Kingfisher Postcards)

Decorated with laurels and flags and with GWR engineers Brunel and Gooch on the footplate, *Lord of the Isles* brought its train into the new Oxford station (not yet open to the public) at 11.10, nearly an hour late. The band of the Life Guards, travelling with the excursion, played awhile as more passengers joined the train, which then set off for the north. At Aynho, its crew passed a disused signal (for a temporary ballast siding) at 'All Clear', thinking it applied to them, and then passed the main line signal (positioned very low anyway) set against them at 'Danger'. Only one of the carriages was fitted with brakes and – although every effort was made – the train could not be stopped quickly.

The local train was busy detaching wagons at Aynho station when the special train was seen approaching at speed on the same line. Its driver at once started his engine to try and get away, but the couplings between the carriages and wagons snapped. The special train crashed into the wagons, smashing one of them to pieces, and knocked them on into the carriages, which were not badly damaged although six passengers in them were cut and bruised. Mr and Mrs Berry, of Upper Heyford, and Elizabeth East, a servant at the King's Arms, Deddington, received head and facial injuries such that they could not continue their journey, but the rest of the passengers were able to do so.

*Lord of the Isles* was badly damaged in the crash, breaking its buffer beam and knocking its front wheels from their frames. The disabled locomotive was put in a siding and Brunel went ahead to Banbury with the engine of the local train and its two carriages. This engine then returned to Aynho to take the excursion on to its destination. It had been intended to run through to Birmingham, picking up more guests, thence returning to Leamington for a celebration at the Royal Hotel However, such was the delay that the special train now went only to Leamington, arriving at 16.00, 'about 180 ladies and gentlemen' taking their seats to eat. Another train brought the guests from Birmingham, who arrived at 17.30.

Having been delayed for over an hour, a sumptuous banquet was then enjoyed. The occasion was presided over by GWR director Mr Henry Simmons from Reading. Congratulatory speeches were delivered for the opening of the new line but, agreeable as the event was, 'the unfortunate occurrence in the morning had lessened the pleasures of the meeting, and everyone felt a degree of regret that so auspicious an event had been marred in such a manner'. The celebration finished at 19.00 and the guests went to Leamington station where their special train awaited them. It departed 'amid the cheering of an immense concourse of people, the band of the Life Guards playing a popular air', it was reported.

Reports of the accident in the national press castigated the GWR directors on several counts. 'It is impossible to imagine an accident more directly resulting from gross carelessness and mismanagement,' said *The Times*. Running the excursion and the local train so close together was the primary cause of the trouble, the newspaper argued. 'With such management nobody could wonder that accidents happen; indeed, they have no right to the name.' Later, the Board of Trade also criticized the GWR over the recklessness it had shown with regard to the timing, speed and formation of the special train, and on the 'chronic unpunctuality of the ordinary train'.

Nevertheless, the new GWR line from Oxford to Birmingham was used as scheduled by public passenger trains from 1 October 1852. (Goods services did not commence until February 1853.) At Oxford, 'a large number of persons congregated to witness the arrival of the first train from Birmingham, which reached the new station about ten o'clock'. With the opening of the new Botley Road station in Oxford, the old station at Folly Bridge became a goods station only (and closed altogether in November 1872). There were now ten new stations beyond Banbury, including Cropredy and Fenny Compton on the original Oxford & Rugby section. At long last the Cherwell Valley railway was well and truly open for business.

# 7　Accidental damage

By October 1852 the Cherwell Valley railway had become a part of an important new GWR main line – a trunk route from London to Birmingham. Trains from London (population 2,362,000 in 1851) departed from the Paddington terminus and shared the GWR's Bristol main line as far as Didcot. Here, they turned away northwards to the university city of Oxford (population 25,522), some sixty-three rail miles from the capital. Travelling on up the Cherwell Valley, trains came to the market town of Banbury (population 8,793), about eighty-six rail miles from London. Further north, through Leamington, they arrived at Birmingham (population 233,000), at a distance of 129 miles from Paddington by the GWR route.

Birmingham was a fast-growing manufacturing centre (already nearly twice as big as Bristol by 1851) and was merging with the nearby town of Wolverhampton (population 120,000) to form a massive conurbation. Beyond lay the Midlands and North-west England, which the GWR eventually penetrated as far as Birkenhead over the lines of other railway companies. Gaining access to this lucrative industrial region was a major prize for the GWR but it was won at some expense: the eighty-two miles of new railway connecting Oxford with the territory north of Wolverhampton cost £6,335,000 in total. At this point, however, it was to be almost five years before the GWR obtained agreements to run through trains as far as Birkenhead.

When the new main line first came into operation, through passenger trains ran from London to Birmingham at express timings of 2 hours 45 minutes, calling only at Oxford and Leamington. Between Oxford and Birmingham, a distance of about sixty-six miles, journey times were 1 hour 45 minutes (express train) and 2 hours 30 minutes (ordinary train). Respective first and second class single fares from Oxford to Birmingham were 14s 6d and 10s 6d (express) and 11s 7d and 8s 8d (ordinary). There were six 'down' (northbound) and five 'up' (southbound) trains on weekdays, and two each way on Sundays (plus, on Sundays only, one more each way between Oxford and Leamington, a distance of about forty-two miles).

The advertised train service in October 1852 included weekday express trains from Oxford to Birmingham at 10.25 and 18.40 and in the opposite direction at 08.00 and 19.30. Between times, there were 'down' stopping trains departing from Oxford at 10.30, 11.35, 13.30 and 15.45, with 'up' stopping trains from Birmingham at 11.30, 15.30 and 17.40. There were no expresses on Sundays, but down trains left Oxford at 09.00 and 11.35 to Birmingham (and at 18.50 to Leamington) with up trains to Oxford from Birmingham at 15.30 and 19.00 (and at 08.00 from Leamington). All the stopping trains offered first and second class accommodation, with a few offering accommodation for third class passengers as well.

The GWR had carried third class passengers by goods train before Gladstone's Railway Act came into force on 1 November 1844. This Act compelled all railway companies to provide at least one train each way each day, at a fare of no more than a penny a mile and a speed of not less than 12mph (including stops, to be made at all stations). As a result, the 'Parliamentary' trains brought rail travel within the means of poorer passengers, who now rode in carriages protected from the weather and provided with seats, instead of open goods trucks. 'Parly' trains ran on the new GWR main line, one each way each day (including Sundays), with third class single fares from Oxford of 3s 6d to Leamington and 5s 5d to Birmingham.

In these ways, the erstwhile rural branch line from Oxford to Banbury was transformed into a trunk line from London to Birmingham. Where there had once been only 'one engine in steam' on a solitary stopping train, there were now numerous daily train movements comprising a mixture of fast and slow trains in both directions. The potential for the growth in traffic to cause problems was soon realized: during the whole of the time the Cherwell Valley railway had been a single line branch, there had not been a solitary casualty, but now that it had become a busy double-track main line, a spate of accidents occurred in quick succession. They were caused by both mechanical failure and human error.

There had, of course, been the *contretemps* at Aynho, involving the locomotive *Lord of the Isles,* prior to the official opening of the line. On that same day (30 Septembe, 1852) there was also a minor mishap at Birmingham, involving another locomotive, named *Sultan.* It had been called out to rescue the disabled special train but had itself left the rails and become embedded in the sand for several hours. Within two days of the public opening, on 3 October, a train from Oxford to Birmingham was delayed at 'Woodstock' station by 'the breaking of some portion of the engine'. It was unable to proceed and a telegraph message was sent to Oxford for a replacement locomotive to take the train on its way.

Apparently, a crowd had gathered on the bridge at Banbury to see the train pass by. It had been due to do so at 12.18, but in the event it did not arrive until 13.30. The crowd's patience was exhausted by this time, yet they could have had longer still to wait – had the locomotive failed elsewhere on the line, calling out another might not have been so easy. It is worth noting that the GWR had, by this date, allowed its early experiments with Cooke and Wheatstone telegraphic equipment to lapse. However, in the autumn of 1850 the GWR had come to an agreement with the Electric Telegraph Company to install a trial line between Oxford and Banbury. This became the model for a general installation in later years.

The value of electric telegraph in summoning assistance on the railway was emphasised in situations where it was lacking. When, on 4 October, another derailment occurred north of Banbury, there was no telegraphic communication available. The locomotive of a southbound train was derailed at Harbury station and there was a long delay before it was back on the tracks. Public awareness of the role of telegraph in raising the alarm in such situations was evidenced by the fact that the train's passengers 'did not choose to remain in the carriages to run the risk of getting smashed, so they stood on the bank for upwards of an hour in the midst of a pelting rain, until the train was ready to proceed'.

After four mishaps in five days, things settled down for a while – but not for long! The next accident claimed the life of the first railwayman on the line. It happened during a period of very wet weather. Indeed, the autumn of 1852 was the wettest for many years. Heavy rain did much damage to the new embankments and cuttings, causing extensive flooding at Kennington, south of Oxford, for instance, which was such that locomotives could not get past and the trains had to be pulled through by horses. Delays on the railway were inevitable in these circumstances and the flooding south of the city was a contributory factor in a fatal crash north of Oxford, at Heyford station, on the evening of Friday 26 November 1852.

An express from London to Birmingham was considerably delayed by the floods at Kennington, but at Oxford station a fresh locomotive was waiting to take the train forward. On the footplate was none other than Driver George Thompson, (who had driven the Oxford-Banbury train in earlier days), with stoker Richard Carpenter. Their train was supposed to depart from Oxford at 17.25 but on this occasion did not do so until 19.14 – nearly two hours late. They quickly had matters in hand, however, and the express was soon speeding northwards at 60mph. Although it was a dark evening, Driver Thompson knew 'the road' like the back of his hand – but he did not know what fate had in store for him!

As the express rounded the falling curve near Heyford, driver and fireman saw that the station signal was set at 'Danger'. Thompson blew the whistle and Carpenter applied the brake, but with only a quarter of a mile in which to stop the train could not be halted in time. In the station a trap had unwittingly been set. A southbound local train (due at 19.07) had pulled in late at 19.20. Before letting it go on its way, George Martin, the stationmaster, had decided that it should pick up a truck or two from the goods shed. To do this, the 'up' local had to reverse across the tracks, where it came to rest with its front end blocking the route of the 'down' express. There was no way a collision could be avoided.

Driver Thompson realized this as his locomotive steamed toward the station, so he jumped from the footplate, leaving fireman Carpenter clinging to the brake. In the minor crash which followed, some of the passengers in both trains were bruised and shaken, although fireman Carpenter was lucky and did not get hurt. Driver Thompson was less fortunate. As he jumped down onto the track, he fell against a point lever which severely injured his head and leg. He was carried into the station where he lay unconscious while Mr Edmund Wilson, surgeon of Steeple Aston, was summoned to tend to his wounds. By the time the surgeon arrived, it was too late to do anything for Thompson, who was dead.

The inquest into the accident was held at the Red Lion inn, Heyford, being opened the next day and then adjourned until Wednesday 1 December. It was presided over by Mr J. Churchill, coroner for the district, with a jury of local men and was attended by Mr D. Gooch (locomotive engineer), Mr G.N. Tyrell (superintendent of the line), and Captain Collard (railway police superintendent) on behalf of the company. A verdict of 'accidental death' was returned on George Thompson, whose widow was granted an allowance of 14s a week by the GWR. In the local press, Thompson was reported to have been 'one of the best men in the Company's service' and 'well known between Oxford and Banbury'.

In later years, there were two accidents on the line at farm level crossings. One took place near Kidlington on 19 December 1853 when a carter was crossing the line with a horse and cart at Park Farm. An express train from Oxford to Birmingham ran into them, smashing the cart and killing the horse, 'driving it about a hundred yards along the line till the poor animal was cut in pieces small enough to lay between the rails and let the engine and carriages pass over it'. It appears that the carter escaped uninjured, but the loss to his employer, Farmer Rouse, was estimated at about £40. 'It was fortunate that the train was not thrown off the rails, or the damage might have been considerable,' said the press.

The other accident took place near Somerton on 18 July 1855 when a carter in the employ of Mr S. Rogers, of Round Hill Farm, was engaged in carrying hay from Fritwell meadow. With his team of four horses, he waited at an 'accommodation road' until a down train had passed and then began to cross the line, but the 16.50 up train from Banbury to Oxford came along almost immediately, 'proceeding at its usual speed'. It knocked the wagon to pieces and killed the shaft-horse, though the other three horses escaped, as did the carter. 'The passengers in the train were very much alarmed,' it was reported, but nothing serious happened to them and the locomotive was not much damaged in the collision.

In 1855 too, Kidlington and Somerton were in the public eye for another reason. New railway stations were opened in both places in that year, increasing the number of intermediate stations on the Oxford-Banbury line from three to five. The new station at Kidlington was designated 'Woodstock Road', and the station which had been so named became 'Kirtlington'. (The new station at Somerton was renamed 'Fritwell & Somerton' from 1907.) As far as Banbury was concerned, the LNWR route to London had been eclipsed by the GWR line, even though it was six miles longer. In 1855 there were eight trains a day to Paddington but only four to Euston (and only two of the latter offered through coaches).

To begin with, the LNWR had done well in the excursion business and in 1851 transported over 2,600 Banburians to London for the Great Exhibition. However, by 1855 the *Banbury Advertiser* was reporting complaints about the slow and uncomfortable excursion trains run by the LNWR. Of course, the GWR was not above reproach at times and on 10 September 1855 one of its own excursions got into difficulty. From Heyford, Woodstock Road and Oxford, this was a special train to Bath and Bristol. Respective return fares were 8s 6d (first class) and 5s

Kidlington Station, *c.*1910. In 1853 a train crashed into a horse and cart near here, killing the horse but fortunately leaving the driver uninjured. (Courtesy of Kingfisher Postcards)

The Great Western Station at Somerton, looking north in around 1910. It was near here that a train from Banbury to Oxford smashed into a cart on a farm crossing in 1855. (Courtesy of Kingfisher Postcards)

A train from Portsmouth to Wolverhampton stops at Banbury in 1960. It is hauled by the 4-6-0 locomotive 6934 *Beachamwell Hall*. In the bay platform, a stopping train for Leamington waits to depart behind 6931 *Aldborough Hall*. (Courtesy of Michael Mensing)

(second class) for the full trip. These prices were good value and the train was well patronized, so that '500 persons availed themselves of it'.

According to *Jackson's Oxford Journal,* the outward journey was 'admirably performed', taking about two and a half hours. Leaving Bristol for the return journey at 19.00, the Cherwell Valley special was preceded by another 'monster excursion train' carrying 1,600 passengers in thirty carriages at a 'slackened pace', which delayed it a great deal – at one point, it had to stop for half an hour. As a result, the trip home took four and a half hours! Nevertheless, in 1857 the *Banbury Guardian* reported on the increasing popularity of excursions by train, notably with the younger generation who often set off on 'jaunts to London, Portsmouth, Manchester or Warwick, without timidity or unnecessary excitement'.

Many rail travellers still feared the possibility of an accident, and there were yet more to come on the Cherwell Valley line. On 28 December 1857 a second railwayman was killed while on the footplate of a locomotive named *Prince,* one of only six of its class. It was racing down Fenny Compton bank with an express from Oxford to Birmingham when a connecting rod broke free and smashed a big hole through the casing of the firebox. The firebox door blew open and escaping steam scalded the footplate crew, who were taken to the Warneford Hospital,

Leamington. The fireman, Frederick Sutton, died from his injuries but the driver, James Bordiss, survived and resumed his career as a train driver.

Details of a lesser accident were recalled in later years by Thomas Houghton Wright, who eventually became a GWR locomotive superintendent. On an unspecified date, the morning express from Birmingham to London suffered a mechanical failure. The train was being hauled by the locomotive *Queen* (another of the *Prince class*) with driver William Thompson and fireman Charles Morkett on the footplate. Near Heyford, the driving axle on the locomotive broke so that a wheel flew off, crossed the line, went through a hedge and into a pool of water. At this, driver Thompson panicked and jumped into the back of the tender, leaving fireman Morkett to apply the brake and bring the express safely to a stand.

Thompson, nicknamed 'Wor Bill' by his mates, gave the impression of having a strong nerve, so his action seemed out of character. His behaviour afterwards was even less credible: the train had been halted by fireman Morkett, but driver Thompson then 'got down and made a fuss before the passengers, who passed round the hat for his bravery in stopping the train, when he had nothing to do with it'. The hapless fireman who was overlooked on this occasion suffered a greater misfortune some time later. Having avoided fatal injury on the railway,

Hall class locomotive 6999 *Capel Dewi Hall* passes through Oxford station on the centre 'road' in 1964 with a freight train for the north. (Courtesy of David Canning)

Charles Morkett died at Slough, being accidentally poisoned 'by taking carbolic acid instead of beer', according to the story told by T.H. Wright.

Traffic using the Oxford-Birmingham line was changing in this period. Since 1852, the third rails laid at the insistence of the Board of Trade to permit the running of narrow-gauge trains had not been used on a regular basis. By 1856, the mixed gauge had been extended south from Oxford and on 22 December of that year the line was first used by a standard-gauge coal train. Standard-gauge goods trains became a common sight between Birmingham and Basingstoke thereafter. Slip coaches, detached from express passenger trains, became another common sight on the line two years later, the first being slipped from the 09.30 Paddington to Birmingham express at Banbury on 29 November 1858.

From 1 May 1857, the GWR started to run through passenger trains between London and Birkenhead – a distance of almost 230 miles. From that year too, the timings of London-Birmingham train services were speeded up. In the summer (May-August) the 09.15 from Paddington reached Birmingham at 12.05, a time of 2 hours 50 minutes. In the autumn (September-October) it was allowed 3 hours, but thereafter more time up to 1859. In that year there was another brief improvement in train timings but subsequently speeds were slackened and by 1864 the GWR's Paddington-Birmingham fast trains were taking 3 hours 20 minutes. The LNWR's Euston-Birmingham trains were allowed just 3 hours for the journey.

With the extension of mixed-gauge track into Paddington, the GWR introduced a new standard-gauge service between London and the north, with three trains each way daily. Only one evening train from Birmingham now remained broad-gauge. The standard-gauge service was entrusted to a class of locomotive unfamiliar on the southern section, although they had been at work in the north since 1855. There were eight of them, numbered from 69 to 76 but without names. The service started on Wednesday 1 May 1861, the inaugural train being the 09.35 Paddington-Birmingham. The train was a remarkable sight, not one of its four-wheeled carriages being the same as any other in size or design.

There was great excitement as the train left Paddington behind locomotive number 75. On the footplate was T.H. Wright, who recalled that 'some of the Broad Gauge bigots wondered whether the train would ever reach its destination'. It was five minutes late reaching Oxford, where there was an engine-change. Locomotive number 76 took over the train and was driven hard to make up time, so that at Leamington a carriage with a 'hot box' had to be detached. Nevertheless, the train arrived at Birmingham only three minutes late, although the hard driving had overheated the locomotive's smokebox and chimney. The standard-gauge service on the line thus began life much as the broad-gauge service had – in trouble!

# 8 Royal progress

Railways were conceived and born before Queen Victoria came to the throne in 1837, but they developed and grew during her reign. Thus the Victorian era really was the 'railway age', and it seems appropriate that Queen Victoria was the first reigning British monarch to travel by rail in this country. Initially, she did so *en route* from Windsor to London, using the Great Western Railway between Slough and Paddington stations. Prince Albert, while her suitor, had used the line in November 1839 on his way back to the Continent and he soon became an enthusiastic and frequent rail traveller. Queen Victoria, who became his wife in May 1840, proved to be a more cautious convert to rail travel.

The Great Western Railway directors assumed it would be only a matter of time before Queen Victoria made a journey by their line, and built a special saloon at their own initiative. This was fortunate in the event, since they only had two days' notice when she at last made up her mind to take to the rails in 1842! Accordingly, on Monday 13 June, the saloon was marshalled – with other vehicles – into a royal train, hauled by the engine *Phlegethon* with Brunel and his locomotive engineer, Daniel Gooch, on the footplate. By this means, Victoria and Albert were transported from Slough to Paddington in a mere twenty-five minutes. Their return journey on Saturday 23 July was also made by rail.

It was the royal couple's desire for a more private family life which led them into longer rail journeys. They established two new royal residences which members of the royal family often visited. One was at Osborne House on the Isle of Wight (from 1844) and the other at Balmoral Castle in Scotland (from 1848). Not surprisingly, the royal journeys between these more distant retreats were made by train, although this involved travelling over the narrow-gauge tracks of several different railway companies as well as the GWR's broad gauge. In this way, Queen Victoria gained 'personal experience of the inconvenience of a break of gauge, of which she had doubtless heard and read much'.

The royal family first encountered the break of gauge on a journey from Balmoral to Osborne in the autumn of 1849. They had to change trains twice, at Gloucester and Basingstoke, from narrow gauge to broad gauge and back again. It is likely that Queen Victoria was 'not amused', although the fact that the royal train marshalled by the GWR now included a 'new and luxurious saloon', recently built, may have been some consolation. However, it cannot have been sufficient to overcome the inconvenience of the break of gauge altogether, because the royal family contrived to avoid the GWR's broad-gauge tracks completely and adopted routes via London for nearly three years thereafter.

Anglo-Scottish royal trains reverted to the Great Western route in 1852. At the end of August, the royal family again travelled from Osborne to Balmoral via Basingstoke and Gloucester, in spite of having to change trains twice. On this occasion, Her Majesty gave orders that the royal train should not be driven at excessive speed on the GWR line. She had been alarmed the previous year when one of the directors told her that 'they had been driving the Train at the rate of 60 miles an hour'. Queen Victoria was always wary of high speed and on the roof of the royal saloon there was a special disc-and-crossbar signal, used to indicate to the locomotive crew that the train's speed was 'too fast' or 'all right'.

Returning from Balmoral on the morning of Tuesday 12 October, a detour was made into North Wales, where the Britannia Tubular Bridge over the Menai Straits had just been opened. While Queen Victoria travelled through the bridge by train, its engineer, Robert Stephenson, escorted Prince Albert and Edward, Prince of Wales, along the top to explain engineering details. With overnight stops, the royal family resumed their trip by a new route. A fortnight earlier, the GWR's line to Birmingham had been opened throughout, and this was the way the royal train made its way southwards. Its journey took it through the Cherwell Valley, whose inhabitants were afforded their first glimpse of royalty.

On Thursday 14 October the royal train used the LNWR line to pass Birmingham, where the Lord Mayor had once offended Queen Victoria by introducing her to the coroner – she is reputed to have remarked that it might be the Sanitary Inspector next! At a bridge over the GWR line, temporary platforms had been set up beside both railways so that the royal party could change from narrow to broad gauge. The Great Western train was hauled by *Lord of the Isles*, now fully repaired after its crash at Aynho prior to the public opening of the line. Brunel was on the footplate once again, and it is reported that he 'took charge of the engine' (though he always denied that he actually did the driving).

The GWR always took special care with royal trains. The company stationed its police, with reinforcements of porters and permanent way men, all along the route of a royal train. A 'pilot' engine was sent off fifteen minutes ahead of the royal train to ensure the way was clear, after which nothing else was allowed onto the line, and all goods trains in the opposite direction were stopped until the special had passed. The chief officers and directors of the company were always in attendance too, as they were on this occasion. Thus, as their train set off through the autumn afternoon, the royal family's safety and comfort were assured in the luxurious Great Western saloon built especially for them.

Constructed around 1848, this saloon had a wooden body mounted on an iron frame built at Swindon. It was over thirty feet long and had a maximum height of 7ft 7in. It featured sides constructed with large plate glass windows and bulges which gave a maximum width of ten feet. There was a large central compartment for the royal family, lavishly furnished in what has been described as 'Victorian-Puritan' style, and smaller compartments at each end, one to accommodate attendants and the other providing toilet facilities. As built, it was an eight-wheel, broad-gauge vehicle, but it was fitted with a pair of bogies and vacuum brakes in 1887 and rebuilt to standard gauge in 1889 (it was finally scrapped in 1903).

Queen Victoria's Great Western royal saloon, constructed around 1848, with its disc-and-crossbar signal for signalling to the footplate crew.

In the Cherwell Valley, loyal subjects had turned out in force all along the line. The royal train was due at Banbury at about 16.40, so the Mayor and Corporation began to assemble at the railway station soon after four o'clock. The interior of the station was decorated with festoons of laurels, evergreens and flowers, while from the walls were suspended banners with inscriptions such as 'God Save the Queen' and 'For God, the Queen, and my Country'. Part of the up (southbound) platform had been cordoned off and covered with a carpet to be used by the borough dignitaries, 'each of whom was permitted to introduce two ladies'. Outside the cordon, a large crowd waited to witness the ceremony.

It had been intended that an address should be read to Her Majesty but this was dispensed with in the event as her train was late and did not arrive at Banbury until almost five o'clock. Instead, the Mayor (Mr E. Bennett) was introduced to the royal family while the corporation presented them with a copy of *Beesley's History of Banbury* and a supply of the far-famed Banbury cakes. It was reported that Queen Victoria and Prince Albert, with their children, stood in the royal saloon and 'kindly acknowledged, by repeated bows, the hearty cheering of the assembly'. As it was now getting dark, the carriages were lighted up and the train was then signalled on its way, having stopped for just six minutes.

The royal train left the station amid loud cheering which 'extended a considerable distance along the line'. At the lineside villages, the train's passing was greeted in similar fashion and Oxford was reached at about half past five. 'Every available position which commanded a view of the line was occupied, and for a considerable distance on both sides were people congregated', according to *Jackson's Oxford Journal*. This was in spite of the fact that the Home Secretary, Mr Spencer Walpole, had been in touch with the city functionaries earlier in the day to inform them that the royal train would not stop at Oxford station and so there would not be any opportunity to present an address to Her Majesty.

Nevertheless, 'an immense number of persons congregated at the Botley Road station to catch a glimpse of the royal party'. That was all the citizens of Oxford got, for the royal train did not stop but merely slowed to about ten miles an hour as it passed through, to the deafening cheers of the assembled multitude. Shortly after passing the station, the train increased speed and disappeared into the darkness. The royal family arrived safely at Windsor (to which a branch line had been opened from Slough in 1849) by quarter to seven that evening. Thus, without problem and to the enthusiastic acclaim of her subjects, no less a person than Queen Victoria made her first trip by train along the Cherwell Valley railway.

The Cherwell Valley route was again used in 1853, although the change for the break of gauge was made at Leamington. Tired of changing trains, the royal family subsequently made their Anglo-Scottish journeys via London each year until 1860. Then the GWR line was sampled again, still via Oxford and Banbury, but changing systems at Bushbury Junction, near Wolverhampton. This permitted narrow-gauge royal trains to make the entire trip – using the GWR's newly laid mixed-gauge tracks – so that Her Majesty no longer needed to change trains. It seems that the narrow-gauge LNWR royal train was used for most of these journeys, running throughout between Balmoral and Gosport (for Osborne) or Windsor.

Thereafter, Queen Victoria regularly made four journeys a year by the Great Western line and the Bushbury link for the rest of her reign. On the Cherwell Valley line, the annual passing of the royal trains was among the highlights of the period. The schedules normally meant that it was late afternoon when the trains reached Banbury – time for high tea! Her Majesty may therefore have appreciated the customary gift of Banbury cakes which were presented to her at the railway station. The GWR built a new saloon in 1874, which was twinned with that of 1848 in royal trains, but in 1897 the former was itself rebuilt and included in a new royal train assembled to mark the Diamond Jubilee of Queen Victoria's reign.

If Queen Victoria was a late and reluctant convert to rail travel, succeeding generations of royals certainly were not. She took her eldest son, Albert Edward (who was born in 1841 and later became Prince of Wales), on his first train journey when aged only eight months. He made his own family home at Marlborough House in London after he married in 1863. His wife was a Danish princess, Alexandra, although he was notorious for his infidelities (and had plenty of time to indulge in such pursuits since he did not become King until aged sixty). While still Prince of Wales he made a number of visits by rail to Oxfordshire's largest and most celebrated stately home – Blenheim Palace at Woodstock.

This estate had been granted to John Churchill (1650-1722), 1st Duke of Marlborough, in recognition of his victory over the French at the Battle of Blenheim in 1704. The palace, designed by John Vanbrugh, took over twenty years to build, not being completed until 1725. By the 1870s it was home to another John Churchill (1822-1883), 7th Duke of Marlborough, who invited Queen Victoria's eldest son to visit Blenheim. The Duke's own eldest son, George (1844-1892), was a contemporary by age of the Prince of Wales. As heir to the estate, George became Marquis of Blandford and eventually the eighth duke, but his younger brother, Lord Randolph, was the more dominant son.

The Prince and Princess of Wales made pre-Christmas visits to Blenheim in this period. According to the *Oxford Times,* the arrival of the royal couple for their first visit on Tuesday 6 December 1870 was 'a red letter day in the annals of Woodstock'. There was no railway station in the town at this date, so the royal train brought them to the most convenient railhead available in the Cherwell Valley. This was Woodstock Road station (opened 1855), located near the village of Kidlington. Coming from London, the royal train was scheduled to arrive here at 16.15, and 'a goodly number of the residents of the surrounding neighbourhood, anxious to catch a glimpse of royalty' were aware of this fact.

Accordingly, a large crowd of local inhabitants gathered on the road bridge which overlooked the station, the approach to which was under the control of Inspector Yates of the County Constabulary. Soon after four o'clock, the Duke of Marlborough arrived in an open carriage drawn by four horses and postilions and a troop of Oxfordshire Yeomanry lined up in the station yard to receive the special guests. At 16.25, a little late, the royal train steamed into the platform. The vehicles behind the locomotive included the royal saloon and two first class carriages. Waiting with the Duke to meet the train were a GWR Superintendent, Mr G.W. Andrews, and the Woodstock Road stationmaster, Mr Frederick Bell.

Immediately the royal couple stepped from their saloon the Duke stepped forward to greet them. He took the Princess by the arm and escorted her through the station and into the yard to his carriage, followed by the rest of the royal party. Outside, the crowd burst into loud cheering upon recognizing the Prince of Wales, who responded by raising his hat to them and smiling graciously. The royal pair, with the Duke, got into his carriage, around which the Yeomanry formed a guard of honour, and it was rapidly driven away to Blenheim, 'amid the huzzas of the spectators'. Their Royal Highnesses returned to London from Woodstock Road station by a special train on Saturday 10 December 1870.

There was another royal visit 'to the splendid domain of Blenheim, in response to an invitation from his Grace the Duke of Marlborough' on Tuesday 9 December 1873. On this occasion the Prince of Wales was accompanied by his younger brother, Prince Alfred, the Duke of Edinburgh, as well as his wife. The royal party travelled from London in private saloon carriages attached to an ordinary fast train which left Paddington at 15.30. This train reached Oxford at 17.24, whereupon the private carriages were detached from the ordinary train. The Princes of Wales and Edinburgh alighted briefly at the station but met no-one, as members of the public were not admitted onto the platform.

A special train was promptly marshalled by coupling the private saloon carriages to their own locomotive and this was despatched from Oxford at 17.26. It made the short journey to Woodstock Road station where it arrived at 17.41. Here, the royal party was met on the platform by the Marquis of Blandford and Lord Randolph Churchill, as representatives of the Duke and Duchess of Marlborough, along with Mr H. Stevens, Superintendent, and Mr Frederick Bell, stationmaster, as representatives of the GWR. Outside the station, the 'C' (Woodstock) troop of the Oxfordshire Yeomanry Cavalry (which included the band) were drawn up in the yard under the command of Captain H. Barnett, MP.

The visit of the Prince and Princess of Wales and the Duke of Edinburgh caused quite a stir in the locality and once again large crowds turned out to witness the proceedings. *Jackson's Oxford Journal* reported of Kidlington itself that the event 'created no little interest in this village when it became known that their Royal Highnesses would alight at the Woodstock Road station'. On the evening concerned, numerous inhabitants of the place gathered around the station approaches to view the royal arrival. On this occasion, the train was punctual and was observed approaching at the expected time. Upon alighting, the royal guests 'were heartily welcomed by the assembled multitude'.

The station had been especially decorated, with drapes on the walls and carpets on the floor. Mr Frederick Bell, described as 'the much-respected Station-master' was an appropriate representative of the parish to greet the royal party. The Marquis of Blandford and Lord Randolph Churchill accompanied their distinguished visitors to the station yard where an open carriage, drawn by four horses driven by postilions, awaited them. The cortège – consisting in all of four carriages with the yeomanry as an escort – set off for Blenheim, being 'loudly cheered on their departure from the station'. The royal party returned to London from Woodstock Road station at noon on Saturday 13 December 1873.

Clearly, in the mid-Victorian period the railway played a major role in bringing members of the royal family before their subjects in the Cherwell Valley. This royal progress was soon curtailed by an unfortunate series of events however. In 1875 the Marquis of Blandford left his wife and eloped with Lady Aylesford while her husband was on a visit to India with the Prince of Wales. Lord Aylesford was obliged to return home, which annoyed the Prince and eventually caused a quarrel between him and Lord Randolph Churchill, who threatened to expose the Prince's private life and so prevent his accession to the throne. The Prince challenged Churchill to a duel but he declined to accept!

In the end, the Prince of Wales demanded – and received – written apologies from both Lord Randolph Churchill and the Duke of Marlborough. He still refused to be seen in the company of Churchill for many years and the family's social life suffered as a result. Moreover, in 1883 Lady Blandford went to court and secured a decree of separation from her husband. The Marquis of Blandford got into debt and quarrelled with Lord Randolph Churchill, so that by 1889 the brothers were not even on speaking terms. The former died in 1892 and the latter (after a brief political career) in 1895. Only then, after more than twenty years, were the Prince and Princess of Wales persuaded to visit Blenheim again.

# 9   Lesser mortals

The world in which ordinary English people lived was experiencing tremendous changes by the mid-nineteenth century. Railways were the prime movers of the rapid progress taking place, which resulted in a high degree of social and geographical mobility for the country's population as a whole. While royalty and other important people might pass through districts opened up by new railways, lesser mortals were also afforded new opportunities for both short- and longer-distance travel. Folk who had never been to the seaside or visited their capital city were now able to visit these and other places.

By all accounts, the Great Western – like other early companies – initially had little time for lesser mortals. In 1839 the company's secretary, Charles Saunders, referred to them as 'the lowest order of passengers', who travelled third class and were not to be encouraged! Around the same date, a Parliamentary Select Committee on Railways reported that the carriages provided by the GWR for its third class passengers were of 'an inferior description'. Trains for third class patrons ran 'at very low speeds', it alleged, and had their passenger carriages combined with 'cattle, horses and empty wagons'.

Hubert Simmons, a GWR stationmaster who served on the Cherwell Valley line at Aynho, claimed that twenty years later it was still the practice to run only one cheap, or third class, train in each direction on most lines. These were the 'Parly' (Parliamentary) trains, which originated from an Act of Parliament in 1844. They were shunted and stopped as often as possible, he wrote in retirement, 'in order to make people pay second class and express fares'. Even though an ex-employee, he condemned the GWR's treatment of lesser mortals; they were not 'entitled to a particle of respect and the third class carriages were little better than cattle trucks'.

Early GWR passenger carriages, whether broad or standard gauge, express or local, were usually small four-wheeled vehicles. When the Birmingham line opened in 1852 a fleet of broad-gauge coaches was introduced with a mixture of first and second class accommodation only. Eight-wheeled and forty feet in length, they were known as 'Long Charleys', being the first such vehicles to see regular use in British express train service. Later, when the through service to Birkenhead started in 1857, the GWR bought 200 standard-gauge, four-wheeled coaches which saw service on the Cherwell Valley line.

Around this time, only three through GWR trains carried third class travellers from Paddington, one of them being the 'Northern Cheap' which left the capital at 07.40 for stations beyond Birmingham. It was not until 1860 that this train was re-timed to leave London at a more reasonable hour, just before midday. Broad-gauge locomotives still ran from Paddington northwards beyond Oxford, although rarely further than Leamington. By the mid-1860s, however, most

A down express train with 6870 *Bodicote Grange* passes through a cutting north of Kidlington in 1865. (Courtesy of Nigel Payne)

passenger trains to and from the north-west were hauled by standard-gauge engines – with a corresponding change in coaching stock, of course.

As far as the company's local trains were concerned, a few catered for lesser mortals but they were rare except between Birmingham and Wolverhampton. Normally there were only one or two daily third class stopping trains running between major stations. This was as true on the Cherwell Valley line as anywhere else on the GWR system. In 1865, for instance, there was still only one all-stations stopping train each way between Oxford and Banbury fully open to third class passengers, the 11.00 from Oxford (08.00 ex-Paddington) and the 15.05 from Banbury (06.40 ex-Birkenhead).

There were other local trains serving Cherwell Valley stations at this time, but not many. Between Oxford and Banbury, the 1865 timetable shows just four stopping trains each way on weekdays (three on Sundays) in each direction. These travelled northwards from Oxford at 08.22, 11.00, 15.55 and 18.40 on weekdays and 09.10, 11.48 and 17.10 on Sundays. Southwards from Banbury they departed at 07.52, 11.22, 15.05 and 19.55 on weekdays and 11.50, 15.20 and 19.45 on Sundays. One train each way carried third class passengers without restriction but use of the others was limited; they were aimed at first and second class travellers.

In the 1860s the Great Western Railway's attitude to lesser mortals was evident from the number of carriages of different classes that it operated. Of the total, there were 270 first and 380 second class, but only 200 third class carriages. Not surprisingly, in an age when the potential third class passenger market was

Hall class loco 7924, named Thornycroft Hall, approaches Oxford Station from the south with a passenger train in 1966. (Courtesy of David Canning)

considerable, the GWR's third class ticket receipts did almost double between 1846 and 1870 – but only from 27% to 45% of all ticket sales. Clearly, the GWR was not keen to cater for third class passengers, instead regarding middle and upper class passengers as its main source of income.

One such patron of GWR trains in the Cherwell Valley was George James Dew (1846-1928). He was born and lived at Lower Heyford, the eldest son of John Dew who ran the family building firm (and the local post office). In adult life, George occupied several administrative posts, mostly in local government, including those of relieving-officer-cum-registrar for the eighteen parishes in the Bletchingdon district of the Bicester Poor Law Union. He compiled diaries which illustrate (among other things) the use he made of the local railway, for both business and pleasure, during the 1860s and 1870s.

Dew's first recorded railway journey, made at the age of fifteen with family and friends, was to London on Friday 8 August 1862. 'G. Dew, J. Dew Senr., J. Dew Junr., E. Dew, Eliz. Dew, Miss Dandridge's Cook & Revd. G. D. Faithfull's Footman went to the International Exhibition'. The trip was made by an excursion train which departed from Heyford station at 07.22 and returned there at 23.40. 'After we left the Exhibition we went to Madame Tussauds'. On the journey they observed 'Windsor Castle very plainly while in the train' and noted that the harvest was 'more forward towards Reading than at Heyford'.

Like Dew, other country folk visited London by means of excursion trains, providing day trips at cheap fares. Thousands saw the capital for the first time in 1851 when they visited the Great Exhibition. There were excursion trains to other cities, to the seaside and countryside or to sporting and social events. On 23 July 1863 George Dew wrote: 'Papa went to Worcester by an Excursion train to see the Royal Agricultural Show. A cheap trip for 2/6'. *En route*, Dew's father 'saw the Malvern Hills'. Excursion trains allowed people to sample pleasures and leisure opportunities not readily accessible to them before.

Country folk generally were slow to realize the life-changing potential of railways and to incorporate train services into their daily routines. Not so George Dew: for most of his life he suffered stomach disorders which led him to seek 'hydropathic' (water) cures at spa towns. This may be the reason for his brief diary note of Saturday 4 March 1865, which simply says, 'Went by the 4.30 train to Leamington', (although he did also have relatives in that spa town). However, he certainly visited the spa at Malvern, Worcestershire, for health reasons during 1865 – when he stayed for three months – and 1866.

These journeys to Worcestershire were also made by train. For example, a diary entry of 13 October 1866 records: 'Saturday. Started for Malvern by the first train from Heyford. And from Oxford at 11.40 am, reaching Malvern a little before 2 pm ...'. Dew must have known that there was spa water to be had closer to home, at King's Sutton. Here, in a meadow near where the village's railway station was opened in 1872, was a little spring whose water tasted like that at Leamington Spa and was supposed to be good for rheumatism. However, it was never much in demand – by Dew or anyone else!

The 4-6-0 loco 6931 *Aldborough Hall* at Banbury in 1960 with the 20.10 service to Leamington Spa. (Courtesy of Michael Mensing)

The diaries also record the use made of the railway by more exalted personages, such as on Monday 1 October 1866: 'Lady Jersey came [to Heyford station] by train between 5 & 6 pm, in the express which stopped for her'. The Jersey family residence was at Middleton Stoney and when the Cherwell Valley line was built their support for the project was secured by the promise of a station at Somerton (opened in 1855). This ploy was frequently used by railway companies to win over influential landowners. However, it seems that the Jersey family found the station at Heyford more convenient most of the time.

Lady Jersey died early in the following year and on Friday 1 February 1867 her body 'came by train this morning to Heyford Station, & was conveyed from hence to Middleton in the hearse in which it came. The bell was tolling for her at the time ...' The next day, Dew recorded that he 'Went to Middleton Park to see the Countess Dowager of Jersey buried'. At the church she was interred in the family vault with other members of the Jersey family, including the 5th Earl and his son, the 6th Earl, (who had died just three weeks after his father). Lady Jersey was grandmother to the young 7th Earl of Jersey.

The most exalted person of all to use the Cherwell Valley railway was, of course, Queen Victoria, and Dew noted certain occasions when she travelled through Heyford. On Friday 30 November 1866, the by now widowed monarch 'passed by us at 11.25 am in a special train drawn by an engine almost covered with flags & other decorations on her way to Wolverhampton for the purpose of opening a statue to the memory of her late husband, the Prince Consort'. Albert, who 'converted' Victoria to the railways, had died a relatively young man on 14 December 1861 and thereafter she travelled alone.

Dew noted another royal excursion through Heyford on Wednesday 17 May 1871: 'The Queen passed here at 9.30 pm in a Train consisting of many carriages'. As usual, a pilot engine 'passed along about a quarter of an hour before the royal train'. Again, on Wednesday 21 May 1879, 'Queen Victoria & suite passed Heyford Station at 9.45 or thereabouts last evening on her way to Balmoral, in a rather long special train which was brilliantly lighted. An engine always precedes her about a quarter of an hour, & the labourers on the line are posted to see that all is right'. This was the standard GWR practice.

To return to lesser mortals, the diaries record other more humble rail trips. Country folk, such as farm workers, had no need to make use of the railways on a regular daily basis (and did not have the money to do so) but there were occasions when a train journey (and the expenditure it entailed) was worthwhile. For instance, on Thursday 17 October 1867, Dew mentioned 'An Excursion Train to Banbury Hiring Fair'. From Heyford station alone 'there went 170 persons'. Many of these would have been farm workers seeking new jobs for the coming year, as most were employed on an annual basis.

In country districts, more regular users of local trains were farmers and others of their class and means, who journeyed to nearby towns for both business and social purposes. A high proportion of such people made use of rural railway services, although the number of daily customers at typical rural railway stations

A branch train at Woodstock with a cargo of milk churns sitting on the platform. The date is pre-1930 and the loco is number 1484. (Courtesy of Mrs R. Giraud)

was low. The average country station was served by only three or four trains each way, most of them stopping at all stations. This was adequate for the infrequent, even if regular, requirements of rural passengers in Victorian times. It was evidently sufficient for the likes of George Dew of Heyford.

Much of Dew's rail travel was for pleasure. On Saturday 21 September 1867, for example, he 'Went to Leamington by the mid-day train on a visit to my cousin Fred'. Just over a year later, on Saturday 31 October, 1868, he enjoyed a train journey on the final day of broad-gauge operations in the Cherwell Valley. 'I rode, for the last time, on this part of the G. W. Railway in a BROAD guage (sic) train', he says of this historic occasion. Writing in his diary a couple of days later, he added that: 'All the trains that run now are narrow guage & the broad guage line is to be taken up'.

As a result of the change of gauge, Dew had cause to make a train journey in an official capacity some time later. In January 1872 he was appointed as smallpox vaccination registration officer for the area, and in the summer of that year encountered the disease, which was 'sadly fatal at Somerton'. The victims were railway workers, being a man named Robert Golder along with two brothers and their father by the name of Andrews. The smallpox 'was caught and brought to Somerton from Wales by the two younger Andrews & Golder ... The elder Andrews caught it in nursing the sons'.

On Saturday 29 June the nurse from Oxford who had been attending the men travelled to Somerton by rail. Dew joined her on the same train at Heyford. At Somerton, they found that the Andrews brothers and their father had died. Dew 'registered the three deaths on the step of the Public House (the Railway Tavern) near the station for they were not willing to let the nurse go in'. Golder, the fourth

The Railway Tavern in Somerton, where Dew recorded the deaths of the Andrews family. The village railway station is just off picture to the right. (Courtesy of Kingfisher Postcards)

man who had the disease, was found in an adjoining house 'sufficiently recovered to be able to walk about'. The men had been 'in the employ of the G. W. Railway in taking up the "Broad gauge" line'.

On a more pleasant note, Dew recorded an outing by rail on Wednesday 2 June 1875: 'In company with Mr Wm. Wing of Steeple Aston I went by an Excursion Train from Heyford Station to Henley on Thames'. This train was hired at a cost of £60 by the Independent Order of Good Templars. At Henley, members marched about 'wearing their regalia'. The return fare from Heyford was 4s, the train leaving from there at 07.30 and getting back at 22.45. A leaflet in Dew's diary shows that his father, John Dew of Heyford Post Office, was one of the agents for the sale of tickets for the excursion train.

'We went to Mr Wing's son's lodgings to have some lunch', wrote Dew, '& then he & a friend of his rowed us down to Medmenham, which lies on the bank of the Thames some four or five miles down, where there are the ruins of a monastery'. The trip back along the river was aided by the weather: 'A brisk wind helped us back to Henley'. Here, they had tea at Mr Wing's son's lodgings, after which there was time to walk up into the hills to 'survey the town'. Finally they made their way to Henley station to catch the train home to Heyford. Dew declared himself 'thoroughly satisfied with the day's enjoyment'.

In March, 1872, Dew married the then headmistress of Lower Heyford school, Miss Mary Banfield, or Polly as he called her. Dew and his wife went on a really adventurous outing on Wednesday 8 July 1879: 'In company with Polly I went by an Excursion Train to Portsmouth'. This train was hired by some people in

Deddington (who must have joined it at Aynho). The Dews' journey started at 04.40, and they did not arrive back until well after midnight, and yet 'many people went from Heyford'. In all, the excursion attracted around four hundred passengers at a return fare (from Heyford) of 5s 6d.

'Spent a very pleasant day', wrote Dew. 'Saw the Dockyard, & went over Nelson's old ship the "Victory", as well as spending two or three hours in Ryde, in the Isle of Wight, the journey to the island being of a most rough kind, the wind blowing a gale the whole of the time'. The outing was just one of many excursions run by the railway to almost every south coast resort between Margate and Weymouth, and it involved the participants in a twenty-hour day, which was not untypical. In spite of this, Dew noted in his diary that they got home 'after spending a pleasant though somewhat tiring day'.

The popularity of the South Coast as a destination for railway excursions is evident from other sources. It was also visited by the employees of Banbury's Britannia Ironworks on the annual August outings of their Recreation Society around this time. In 1877, some 700 Banburians entrained to Portsmouth, many of them having never before seen the sea! In the next year, 800 set out by train at 06.40 and were astonished to be afloat off the Needles by lunchtime, the *Banbury Guardian* reported. In 1880, 1,200 went to Weymouth and saw the yacht belonging to Bernhard Samuelson, their employer.

Journeys by railway excursions were, of course, special events in the lives of lesser mortals. Normally, they would only have used the train to visit a nearby town or village, and probably only then for a specific reason. For example, when girls entered domestic service (the second largest occupation in the mid-nineteenth century), they often went by train, as 'their fathers pushed their boxes on wheelbarrows to the railway station'. However, for most ordinary folk, it has been suggested, the rural railway was used 'almost exclusively as a local amenity, rather than as a means of leaving the area'.

Nevertheless, there were times when country people did use the railway to leave the area. A depression in agriculture in the 1870s and 1880s caused many thousands of rural labourers to emigrate. *Jackson's Oxford Journal* described a local exodus via Banbury on 16 March 1887. 'On Wednesday morning, upwards of 60 emigrants left the Great Western Railway Station for Liverpool, *en route* for America', it reported. They came from several villages in the area around the town, including Ratley, Warmington, Sibford, Epwell, Middleton Cheney, Chacombe, Farthinghoe, Souldern and Deddington.

During the Victorian period, rural railways revolutionized the social habits and outlook of country folk. It soon became clear that, of all the classes in the community, the railway most benefited the poor. The growth in third class travel was spectacular: in 1846, it accounted for less than half of all passenger travel but, by 1870, it was up to two-thirds. By 1890 the proportion of passengers travelling third class was around 96%. Where once rural people rarely went far from the villages where they were born, railways made them more mobile. As the years passed, lesser mortals were increasingly on the move!

# 10   A frightful smash

In retirement, the GWR stationmaster Hubert Simmons showed his disdain for the company which had once employed him by referring to it as the 'Great Smash Railway'. By the time of his retirement, at the end of the third quarter of the nineteenth century, the epithet seemed warranted, but for most of the time he was in the company's service it was not. The Great Western had coped with a huge increase in traffic and become one of the largest railway companies in the country, but fortunately suffered relatively few serious accidents. In the eight years from 1866 to 1873 inclusive, only one passenger had been killed in a crash on the company's trains. Then, in 1874, three bad accidents occurred on the GWR, at West Drayton, Merthyr Tydfil and Hampton Gay, the latter – on Christmas Eve – being described as 'the blackest day in Great Western annals'.

The outside world was linked to Hampton Gay from the east by a dead-end road but a great meander in the River Cherwell prevented other direct road communication. On the river was an ancient water mill which ground corn until it was converted to a paper mill in 1681. Close by was the manor house, rebuilt by the Barry family in the Elizabethan period, along with the little medieval church, also rebuilt (in 1767-1972) and dedicated to St Giles. The parish was the smallest in the area – its population peaked at eighty-six inhabitants in 1821 and declined thereafter. Thirty years later, the railway sliced through the hamlet and the church found itself right beside the line. By 1874, the manor house was shared between two tenants, one of whom was Robert Langton Pearson, a papermaker who leased the mill and employed several men there. As they began work early on Thursday 24 December, none could have imagined how the day would end.

It was a 'White Christmas', bitterly cold, with frost and snow on the ground and four inches of ice on the Oxford Canal. In the capital, at Paddington, some seventy miles away by rail, throngs of passengers boarded trains, intent on spending the holiday with family and friends. The 10.00 London to Birkenhead express was very crowded when it set out, even though it had been lengthened to thirteen carriages, and when it stopped at Reading yet another carriage was added to cope with the demand for seats. The increasing delay resulted in its late arrival at Oxford – where it was due at 11.35 – so that it did not pull into the platform until 12.06. Here, too, the number of waiting passengers meant that further accommodation would have to be provided.

The only thing the Oxford stationmaster, James Gibbs, had available was an elderly coach (number 845), originally built for the Newport, Abergavenny & Hereford Railway. Unlike the fourteen vehicles already making up the train, which were six-wheeled first and second class stock, this extra coach was a small, four-wheeled, third class vehicle. The locomotive (number 386) that had brought the express from London came off, the extra coach was put on the front of the train, and another locomotive (number 478), which had arrived earlier in the day from Wolverhampton, was put on to resume the journey northwards. At the same time a 'lad' was employed in connecting up the Harrison (communication) cord from the coaches to the locomotive, where it would sound a warning gong if pulled in an emergency – but he failed to do his job properly.

Meanwhile, a huddled conference was taking place on the platform. The district locomotive foreman, Garlick by name, was concerned that locomotive 478 was incapable of hauling such a heavy train over Hatton Bank, beyond Leamington, on its own (especially if, as seemed likely, even more coaches might be added further along the line). He advised stationmaster Gibbs that it would require the assistance of locomotive 386 to ensure that the express continued on its way without further loss of time. The two locomotives were of the same class, designed by the GWR's locomotive superintendent, Joseph Armstrong, of which thirty were built at Swindon between 1866 and 1869. All were six-wheeled locomotives with a single pair of 7ft driving wheels and were regarded as 'powerful engines' in their day, doing an immense amount of work.

Thus, at 12.15 (after a stop of only nine minutes) a double-headed leviathan steamed away from Oxford station. The Birkenhead express now consisted of fifteen coaches carrying around 500 passengers, a considerable challenge for the two engine crews trying to get their load moving at speed on slippery rails. On number 386, the 'pilot' (front) locomotive, based at Oxford, were driver William Butler and fireman William Money, who had already worked the train down from Paddington. On number 478, the 'train' (rear) locomotive, based at Wolverhampton, were driver Henry Richardson and fireman James Hill, who had worked another train in from the north that morning. A regular express driver from Wolverhampton shed, Richardson, now aged fifty-three, had been promoted to 'Engineman First Class' in 1854, at the then princely wage of 7s 6d per week.

Hard at work, the engine crews had their train moving at about 35mph as it thundered through Woodstock Road station (Kidlington). There, stationmaster Frederick Bell was standing on the down platform awaiting the arrival of the 'Cheap' stopping train, itself running late having been held at Oxford until the express had left. Bell glanced at his pocket watch as the express passed – 'to all appearances in proper condition' – at 12.26. Unbeknown to him, however, all was not well and disaster struck just two minutes later. In the extreme cold, the metal tyre on the right-hand leading wheel of the third class coach was fracturing. On the straight stretch of line beyond Kidlington, where the express began to accelerate, the tyre finally disintegrated, taking with it part of the iron wheel. The little coach became derailed, but the train steamed on regardless.

This took place a mile and a quarter north of Kidlington, near Hampton Gay. Busy on their engines, the crews were at first unaware of the mishap. Then, on the footplate of number 478, driver Richardson noticed the clapper of the alarm

Looking north along Kidlington's down side platform, *c*.1935. The fated Birkenhead express ran through on the adjacent track.

gong moving, although not enough to ring it. He looked over the side of his engine, back along the train, and was astonished to see 'a fountain of snow and ballast flying up from behind the tender'. Next, fireman Hill looked back along the train and saw a passenger leaning out of a coach window, waving his arms and calling 'Whoa! Whoa!' Richardson blew his locomotive's deep-toned alarm whistle to alert the crew of the locomotive in front and the guards in the train behind to apply their brakes. At once, both drivers shut off steam and reversed their engines while the firemen screwed down their tender brakes.

In the circumstances, this was the *worst* action they could have taken. Until then, the train had continued to run with all the coaches remaining upright because of the tension of the couplings. If stopped gradually, the train might have been saved, but the sudden brake application at its head (with no corresponding braking at its rear) simply resulted in a 'concertina' effect. The momentum of the fourteen unbraked six-wheelers running on behind crushed the crippled four-wheeler and forced it to swerve to the left about halfway along the 200 yards of track between the river and canal bridges. It crashed down the embankment into a meadow some twenty feet below, where it was 'smashed to atoms'. The next nine coaches also careered off the track to left and right so that only the last five remained upright, and three of these were derailed.

The down platform at Bletchington station, where William Butler arrived with his locomotive on Christmas Eve 1874 bringing news of the crash at Hampton Gay. (Courtesy of the *Oxford Mail*)

The two locomotives, freed from the train, cleared the canal bridge before stopping. There was now a danger that approaching trains might hit the wreckage and action had to be taken to prevent this. William Butler, on number 386, the pilot engine, drove forward to Kirtlington (Bletchington) station to raise the alarm there, while William Price, the head guard, accompanied by two passengers, ran back along the line to Woodstock Road station to do likewise. He only just got there in time: by now it was 12.50, and the 'Cheap' stopping train (due at 12.07) was at the station and about to leave. Frederick Bell saw Price coming and ran to meet him. Price said 'You must telegraph to Oxford at once; there is a frightful accident, and we must get assistance from Oxford'. Bell promptly countermanded the order for the 'Cheap' to depart.

Stationmaster Bell immediately sent out six workmen plus a porter – all the staff he could spare from the station – and then got the passengers off the 'Cheap', sending the train down the line to 'bring the wounded to Oxford'. He could not leave the station himself but sent for medical help from the neighbourhood and then ran to the station's telegraph office to get a message through to Oxford station. Unfortunately, the telegraph was faulty – 'the wires were disarranged' – and Bell could not get through to Oxford, though he continued to work the instruments. William Hopkins, telegraphist at Oxford, began receiving the message at 13.10 and it took six minutes to complete: 'From Bell, Woodstock, to Gibbs, Oxford. Frightful accident to down express, near Kidlington. Bring all medical men and all help possible. Very urgent, both lines blocked'.

Fortunately, there was help closer at hand. An Oxford surgeon, Mr H.P. Mallam, was attending Mr Joseph Prior of Shipton House for a broken leg, and was at the scene of the crash within minutes. He was soon assisted by Mr Parry, of Kidlington, and other doctors including a young surgeon from Guy's Hospital who had been a passenger on the train. From Blenheim, Lord Randolph Churchill and several ladies of the Duke of Marlborough's family came with 'nourishment and cordials'. At Hampton Gay, Mr R.L. Pearson directed his employees to help to extricate the passengers from the wreckage. The dead were placed in a storeroom at the paper mill, which became a temporary mortuary, while the injured were carried to the manor house, drafted into use as a makeshift hospital where Mr Pearson's family tore up their linen to make bandages.

At Oxford, Stationmaster Gibbs was handed the dramatic telegram, his first notification of the tragic accident, at 13.20. He quickly organized a special train,

The remains of the manor house at Hampton Gay, which became a makeshift hospital after the accident. The house was burned out in a fire in 1887.

The ruins of the paper mill that served as a mortuary. Twenty-six people were laid out here after the Hampton Gay smash, before being removed to Oxford.

which left Oxford at 13.50 and arrived at Woodstock Road at 14.05. Here, Gibbs 'blocked the road' to other trains and proceeded to Hampton Gay, arriving at 14.10. The scene was one of devastation. For 300 yards approaching the crash site, the sleepers were scored or actually cut in two by the damaged coach, the wheels of which had cut a deep trench where it ran down the embankment. Other coaches also lay 'wheels upward' at the bottom of the embankment with fragments from them covering the meadow and canal. One, which had hit the bridge, 'was so completely ruined that the roof and lamps laid mixed up with the wheels and bottom of the carriage in dire confusion'.

Several coaches, lying on their sides, carried evidence of the injuries their occupants had sustained. 'One end of a first class was crumpled up, and the ghastly stains of blood on the yellow roof, the cushions and the floor testify to the terrible tragedy which was enacted therein'. The crash site was littered with wood splinters, springs, lamps, glass, iron bars and bolts; the 'wonderful confusion of the wreck, which so amazes, while it cannot be described, the shrieks of the wounded, and the wintriness of the scene combined to fix a life-long impression upon those who had the misfortune to be on the spot', it was reported. 'So utterly complete was the ruin of some of the carriages that the first thought which strikes the mind is not that there were so many killed outright, but so few, considering the large number there were in the train'.

Nevertheless, a search of the wreckage revealed that the number of casualties was indeed high. 'Those less severely injured, on recovering from their bewilderment and the sadness of the shock, at once set to work to extricate both the living and the dead. Underneath the floor of a carriage which laid wheels upwards, no less than thirteen dead bodies were removed, all shockingly mutilated'. Before long, twice that number were laid out in the paper mill at Hampton Gay. Four of the seriously injured were transported to Oxford but died before reaching hospital and four more died later, making the total death toll thirty-four. Another sixty-five, including four GWR employees, were badly injured. Fifty-one were hospitalized at the Radcliffe Infirmary, the remainder being treated at New College and at the Randolph, Clarendon, King's Arms and Jones's Railway hotels.

At Woodstock Road station, a journalist from *Jackson's Oxford Journal* used the station's telegraph to send a brief account of the crash to his editor: 'Kidlington, 3.35 pm, Thursday,' it began, 'by electric telegraph – from our own reporter'. It was published on Saturday under the headline 'Latest Intelligence. Frightful Accident on the Great Western Railway near Kidlington'

As darkness fell at Hampton Gay that Christmas Eve, the abundance of timber from the wreckage was used to light fires between the tracks and on the embankment and a limited amount of tidying up was undertaken. Both the up and down tracks were cleared of debris later that evening (only one new rail needed to be fitted) and the line was reopened to traffic. However, most of the

A successor of the wrecked train, the 16.10 Birkenhead express of 14 August 1952 is hauled by loco 6011 *King James I*. Cropredy station can be seen in the distance. (Courtesy of R.H.G. Simpson)

wreckage of the Birkenhead express lay scattered around the site for another three days.

The next day, Friday, was Christmas Day but that did not deter the vast crowds of people 'from Oxford and the villages adjacent' who came to inspect 'the fatal spot', reported *Jackson's Oxford Journal,* whose journalist was back to develop his story. In spite of the presence of police, some people still 'clambered to the top of overturned carriages and peered down through the windows, or searched amid the confused and piled remains'. The 'crimsoned snow' on the embankment near a first class coach 'told terribly what was to be expected of an inspection of the carriage'. In one compartment, 'blood and brains were bespattered all over the interior, interspersed with portions of human hair, and on the floor, amid the wreck of wood and torn cushions, the broken glass lay stiffly frozen in blood, and remained so until Saturday'.

Also on the spot that day was an artist from the *Illustrated London News.* Having made drawings at the site of the crash, he walked to the paper mill. 'I went down a path of slush and mire to a range of low buildings, where the most painful part of my duty was to be accomplished', he wrote. Passing a policeman at the door, he entered the gloomy storeroom and saw twenty-six 'mutilated corpses lying in grim array on their beds of straw, awaiting identification for the inquest before their removal'. The artist's impression of the scene was the cover picture of the next week's *News,* and showed the parents of 'a young and handsome youth of twenty-one years' mourning the untimely death of their son. When all the bodies had been identified, they were placed in coffins by Oxford undertaker Mr Henry Symonds and eight of his assistants and later sent to Oxford.

Oxford station was the site of an inquest hearing after the accident, opened by coroner William Brunner on 28 December 1874. This view dates from around 1910. (Courtesy of Kingfisher Postcards)

On the Saturday, Boxing Day, the Oxford Coroner, Mr William Brunner, came to Hampton Gay. In the drawing room of the manor house, he opened an inquest into the deaths and – with the jurors – inspected the bodies. The inquest was adjourned until Monday, when he opened a further hearing in the first class waiting room at Oxford station for the eight dead there. In the meantime, on the Sunday – when there were few other trains – the Great Western Railway sent hundreds of men, with three or four steam cranes and several powerful jacks, to clear the wreck site. They worked almost uninterruptedly and by nightfall the last of the wreckage had been transported to Oxford station and placed in the goods shed there. 'The third class carriage, which was put on at Oxford, or rather, what remained of it, was placed by itself', it was reported.

After Monday, the two coroner's inquests were combined, and both juries sat with Mr Brunner at County Hall. The inquiry went on well into the New Year. The coroner heard statements from thirty-four witnesses (all but two of whom were GWR employees) and some were cross-examined by solicitors acting on behalf of relatives of the dead. The crash victims came from places as far apart as London and Wolverhampton, Leicester and Wrexham. They included four local people: Mrs Mary White, a lodging house keeper from New Inn Hall Street, Oxford; Edward Sylvester, a city accountant; Samuel Busbridge, a postmaster from Curbridge; and Richard Cartwright, a farm labourer from Launton. The inquiry lasted a total of twelve days and concluded on 16 March 1875, when the juries returned a verdict deciding that the deaths were an 'accident'.

As with any railway disaster, the Board of Trade held a court of inquiry, under its inspector, Colonel Yolland, intended to establish the cause of the accident rather than that of the deaths. It reported in April and concurred with many of the recommendations made by the coroner's court. The engine crews were absolved from blame, though it was pointed out that their (understandable) reaction in stopping quickly had done more harm than good. Instead, the GWR management was criticised on several counts: for failing to issue guidance about how to stop a train in such a dire emergency (as a result of this rebuke, a new rule soon appeared in the 'GWR Rule Book'); for using inefficient communication between the train and its locomotives, (the defective Harrison cord); and for the train's disorganized formation of coaches and inadequate braking power.

Of course, the chief culprit had been the elderly four-wheeled coach. Mr Brunner's inquest juries concluded that the accident had been 'caused primarily by the influence of the atmosphere on the wheel of the third class carriage No. 845'. The extreme cold had certainly played a part in the disintegration of the coach wheel, but Colonel Yolland's inquiry discovered that there was more to it than this. The coach's tyres had been fixed to the wheels by means of countersunk rivets through their rims – the term 'slipshod' is literally appropriate to this technique. The GWR had agreed to abandon it back in 1855, but the little coach had in fact been retyred in this way as recently as 1868. This improvised repair was the root cause of the crash. Ironically, the Great Western had virtually given it up, precisely because it had resulted in so many accidents!

The churchyard of St Giles at Hampton Gay. The gravestone is that of Benjamin Taylor, who died in the crash of 1874. The fateful railway line can be seen in the background.

At Hampton Gay paper mill, the men were reluctant 'to remain on the premises' and Mr Pearson declared himself 'thoroughly unnerved' and in need of 'a change of scene now the excitement is over'. Eventually, he gave up his tenancy and moved away, the mill and manor being taken over by papermakers J. & B. New. On Friday 29 April 1887, the manor house was destroyed in a fire, inevitably giving rise to tales of a curse and hauntings (more credible speculation concerned Messrs. J. & B. New's recent bankruptcy!). Today, St Giles' church stands alone, like a silent sentinel beside the ruins of the manor and mill. In its graveyard is the only tangible reminder of the crash, a headstone dedicated to nineteen-year-old Benjamin Taylor of Wolverhampton who died here in the Cherwell Valley, just one of the thirty-four victims of the worst accident in GWR history.

# 11    Branching out

In the last quarter of the nineteenth century, most of Britain's trunk lines were completed and development focused instead on infilling, with lines branching out to those towns and villages which lay between the main routes. The years from 1873 to 1896 have gone down in history as the 'Great Depression' but in this period rail traffic continued to grow and many more miles of track were built. Britain's total route mileage increased from 15,537 in 1870 to 20,073 by 1890. Branch lines were constructed all over the country, either to serve outlying communities – an unjustified expenditure in the case of little-trafficked areas – or to act as feeders, bringing extra passengers and goods onto the main lines themselves.

By this time, the 'Railway Mania' was over and the railway companies were too financially committed to undertake this work themselves. Even those places which had resisted the coming of the railway a generation earlier now realised their advantages; for instance, the price of coal in most localities dropped by a third when it was brought in by train. Thus, the initiative to promote and construct branch railways was left to local people – landlords, millowners and merchants – although the main line railway companies often waited in the wings to buy up completed branch lines when built, once they were financially viable. So it was when the Great Western Railway began to branch out from its original main line through the Cherwell Valley.

The first initiative came at the northern end of the line, near Banbury, and took many years coming to fruition. In fact, plans to build a branch from Banbury were mooted within months of the opening of the line from Oxford, itself only a branch line at the time! An 'Important Railway Meeting' was held at the Red Lion in the town on Monday 21 April 1851, the *Banbury Guardian* reported, with the aim of promoting a rail link westward from Banbury to connect near Moreton-in-Marsh with the Oxford, Worcester & Wolverhampton Railway. The meeting was chaired by Lord Duncan, who represented the interests of Shipston-on-Stour, which would be served by the proposed railway and so overcome its isolation.

This proposal came to nought but there were interested parties in other places who were keen to have rail links with the wider world. Chipping Norton had been a wool town since the fifteenth century and later developed a cloth industry. In 1821 the firm of Bliss & Son had started tweed manufacture and William Bliss, a far-sighted Baptist mill-owner who realised the advantages of rail transport, began campaigning for a branch line to the place in about 1853. He had earlier agitated for the OW&W to open a station at Bledington, on its Oxford to Worcester main line, to serve Chipping Norton, but when this approach failed he became the prime mover in getting a branch line to the town, from the OW&W main line, built instead.

The Chipping Norton branch line was opened on 10 August 1855, 'from a junction with the main line situated midway between Shipston and Adlestrop stations, where a house has been erected for the issue of tickets to passengers, etc'. The $4\frac{1}{2}$ mile branch was built at a total cost of £26,000 of which local people contributed £10,000 and the contractor (Sir Samuel Morton Peto) the balance. It was operated by the OW&W and bought by that company in 1859. From Chipping Norton Junction station (re-named Kingham in 1909), a branch line to Bourton-on-the-Water was opened on 1 March 1862. These two branches were the basis of a more ambitious project promoted by the GWR – the Banbury & Cheltenham Direct Railway.

After several false starts by other schemes, the Great Western successfully secured an Act of Parliament for its proposed line on 21 July 1873. The prospectus for the B&CD railway said its aim was to link the Eastern Counties with the West of England, importing coal and cattle from Wales and Hereford and exporting iron ore to South Wales. The GWR undertook to work the line 'in perpetuity'. Land was purchased for the building of stations at Adderbury, Bloxham and Hook Norton (at the Banbury end) plus others at the Cheltenham end, and £35,000 earmarked for their construction and for the improvement of Chipping Norton and Bourton-on-the-Water stations. Land was also bought for the line itself and the first sod was cut in 1874.

The eastern section was to join the GWR's Oxford-Banbury main line some three miles south of the latter town at Kings Sutton, where the company had already built and opened a new station at what would become the junction on 1 June 1872. Construction was sufficiently advanced to allow goods traffic to be handled at Adderbury and Bloxham stations by 1877 but work had to be suspended because of the financial crisis of 1878. It was not resumed until the autumn of 1879, when priority was given to the western section, which opened to traffic on 1 June 1881. In that year too, at a cost of £25,000, Parliament approved a change in the route of the eastern section, so that it ran through Hook Norton rather than Swerford.

This proved a challenge for the line's engineer, Mr William Wilson, of Dean's Yard, Westminster. In order to cut down the time involved in building an open cutting across an escarpment and two deep valleys west of Hook Norton, the track was carried over a pair of high viaducts and through a 490 yard long tunnel. Each viaduct consisted of massive stone piers supporting 100ft iron girder spans. One consisted of eight spans carrying the rails 85ft above the valley bottom, the other of five spans at a height of 60ft. For four years, 400 men laboured on them, two falling to their deaths during construction, but when completed the viaducts 'attracted much attention in the neighbourhood, being the only piece of engineering of the kind in the locality'.

Beyond Hook Norton, the line climbed on a gradient of 1 in 100, reaching its summit level 600ft up in the Cotswolds before dropping from the Swere Valley on a gradient of 1 in 80 into Chipping Norton. Heavy earthworks were required here,

Hook Norton station, *c*.1920. The avoiding lines passing to the right of the station gave access to a local ironstone quarry. (Courtesy of Kingfisher Postcards)

The second viaduct on the B&CD line near Hook Norton. Two workmen fell to their deaths during the construction of these aqueducts. (Courtesy of R.H.G. Simpson

Chipping Norton railway station, *c*.1900. A branch terminus was built here in 1855 but this station replaced it after the B&CDR opened throughout in 1887. (Courtesy of Kingfisher Postcards)

Kings Sutton station looking south, *c*.1960. This station was the first one south of Banbury and did not open until 1872. It escaped the Beeching axe and is still open today. (Courtesy of Lens of Sutton)

including another tunnel 750yds long, 10ft wide and 20ft high under high ground immediately before Chipping Norton station, nineteen miles from Banbury by rail. On a sharp curve outside the tunnel a new station, with a splendid GWR standard style goods shed, was built on the B&CD line, leaving the erstwhile terminus station isolated. (It eventually became part of the goods yard and among its sidings was one serving the mills of William Bliss, who had promoted the original branch.)

The B&CD railway left the Cherwell Valley railway at Kings Sutton station (characterised by its decorative stonework and ornate chimneys) at a junction facing Banbury. Another link facing Oxford was authorised but never built. The line was double track to Adderbury and then single track to Chipping Norton. At Adderbury, the building of a station was not originally thought worthwhile, the village being so near the junction, but one was built by the time the line opened, in anticipation of a considerable traffic in iron ore. For this reason too, Adderbury, Bloxham and Hook Norton stations were provided with adequate sidings and passing loops. All three were built of red brick to a similar design and with almost identical goods sheds.

The Banbury and Cheltenham Direct Railway finally opened for passengers on Wednesday 6 April, 1887. 'There was no public demonstration of any kind to celebrate the occasion,' according to the *Banbury Guardian*, although it declared that the new line was 'fairly well patronised' on its opening day and might have

Adderbury station looking east, *c.*1920. This was the first station on the B&CDR line after leaving the Cherwell Valley main line at Kings Sutton. (Courtesy of Lens of Sutton)

Adderbury station, with a distant view of loco 5404 approaching. This locomotive was a regular on the branch line service, hauling an autocoach. (Courtesy of R.H.G. Simpson)

been more so 'if longer notice of the opening of the line had been given' (it was only announced the day before). However, it is on record that at Bloxham, for instance, 'the whole village turned out to see the first train arrive'. Here, the first ticket at the station was purchased by fourteen-year-old George Manning, who set off with his younger brother by train to Kings Sutton, from where they 'drove a pig home'.

The first train comprised an engine and four coaches, catering for three classes. There were four trains each way daily, except Sundays, and passengers travelling throughout between Banbury and Cheltenham saved fifty-one miles on the existing route. However, it was neither for passenger nor for coal traffic that the new section of line chiefly catered, but iron ore. The region between Banbury and Chipping Norton was mostly farmland before the railway opened but there were drastic changes to the landscape as quarrying started up in the fields beside the line. Extensive sidings, narrow-gauge tramways and calcining kilns were built, first at Hook Norton in 1889 and later at places like Adderbury, Bloxham, Milton, Sydenham and Astrop.

The second initiative came at the southern end of the line, near Oxford, and came to fruition more quickly. It involved the building of a short branch line from Woodstock to join the Cherwell Valley line beyond Kidlington. By the late nineteenth century, the ancient town of Woodstock was in decline but its wealthy resident landlord at Blenheim Palace – George Charles Spencer Churchill, the 8th Duke of Marlborough – was its benefactor as far as railway communication was concerned. His father, the 7th Duke, had approached the GWR in 1882 with a view to securing the construction of a branch line, but to no avail. After the 7th Duke died in 1883, the 8th Duke became the prime mover in getting the railway to serve the town.

In 1885 a survey was carried out by Thomas Berwick and a $2\frac{1}{2}$ mile branch was projected from Woodstock to a proposed junction on the GWR main line at Shipton-on-Cherwell (close to the place where, just ten years earlier, the 'frightful accident' had occurred). At Woodstock, a terminus station was planned in the parish of Hensington (fronting the Oxford-Chipping Norton road, across which lay Blenheim Palace) and the tenants occupying one of the town's medieval burgage plots would have to be displaced to make way for it. For most of its route, the projected line was on land owned by the Blenheim Estates. As required by law, plans of the proposed line were deposited with the relevant authorities in the places affected.

Early in 1886 a Bill was presented to Parliament which culminated in the passing of the Woodstock Railway Act on 25 September of that year. The Act contained numerous clauses regarding the building and working of the branch line, most of which were mere legal formalities, but – in what was later to prove an unfortunate oversight – it neglected to deal with the matter of running powers over the main line. Under the terms of the Act, a Woodstock Railway Company was incorporated and authorised to raise capital in the form of £30,000 in shares and £10,000 in loans. Five directors were appointed, one of whom was the Duke of Marlborough. In a separate agreement the same year, the GWR undertook to operate trains over the branch.

The first board meeting of the Woodstock Railway Company was held on 24 February 1888 at 37, Great George Street, Westminster. It was chaired by the Duke of Marlborough but the venue was the headquarters of the railway contractors Messrs Lucas & Aird, who actually seem to have been involved in the scheme from the outset. They were awarded the contract to build the branch line and, interestingly, were to be paid not in cash but in shares! Messrs Lucas & Aird appear to have exercised considerable control over the Woodstock Railway Company's fortunes – at an 'extraordinary meeting' held at 37 Great George Street on 26 March 1889 the directors agreed to raise a further £10,000 by the creation of debenture shares.

Construction of the Woodstock Railway began in 1888, preliminary work being carried out in March and the heavier work commencing in April. Navvies in the employ of Messrs Lucas & Aird took up residence in the locality and on 31 March the *Oxford Chronicle* reported that empty houses in Woodstock 'are being rapidly occupied, and lodging-house keepers are rapidly filling up their vacant beds and apartments'. The engineering work proceeded quickly. Within a couple of months temporary rails 'for the conveyance of materials, etc.' had been laid the length of the line and 'the greater portion of the fencing' erected. 'We understand that the building of the station will be commenced in about two month's time', it was further reported.

Kidlington station (formerly Woodstock Road) in around 1935. The station staff frequently won prizes for the way they maintained the station gardens.

However, something happened to delay the opening of the branch, and a year later the *Oxford Chronicle* was wondering why. On 4 May 1889 it reported: 'One or two conflicting rumours are afloat as to when and how this undertaking will be completed, but in the absence of any direct corroboration it would be premature to say further. One thing is certain, that very nearly all the hands have been discharged and little progress is being made, and whether or not there will be railway communication opened from the town to Oxford this year is an open question'. In fact, the branch line did not open until another year had elapsed for the simple reason that the nature of the junction with the main line had become a contentious issue.

As originally conceived, the Woodstock Railway was intended to connect with the Great Western at Shipton-on-Cherwell by means of a junction and then utilise the tracks of the latter company so that its trains might reach Woodstock Road (Kidlington). The GWR subsequently decided that it could not permit branch trains to run on the main line This problem had been raised at its board meeting in November, 1888, at which its General Manager placed the blame for the difficulty squarely, if rather unfairly, on the Woodstock Railway Company. Instead

Kidlington down side platform in March 1963. This platform was extended as part of the construction of the Woodstock branch in 1889-1890. (Courtesy of the *Oxford Mail*)

of a junction at Shipton, the GWR now required an extension of the branch line alongside the main line so that Woodstock trains could run 'directly into the Woodstock Road station'.

The extra cost this additional work involved was beyond the means of the Woodstock Railway Company and in the end the Great Western itself undertook to finance the extension in return for a share of the traffic receipts once the line was opened. This was on top of what the GWR was already due for operating trains on the branch, resulting in a total payment from the Woodstock Company of £1,240 per annum. The extra work involved laying the permanent way from Shipton to Kidlington and extending the down platform at Woodstock Road station by 300ft to create a branch bay platform. It was carried out by Messrs Lucas & Aird, under the guidance of a GWR engineer, between the autumn of 1889 and the spring of 1890.

On 21 March the Woodstock Railway Company instructed its secretary to write to the contractors urging them to have the line ready in time for the Oxfordshire Show in early May. By then the new line was not quite ready although it was 'rapidly drawing towards completion', reported *Jackson's Oxford Journal*. On 24

Woodstock station and garden, *c*.1910. The two bogie clerestory coaches in the siding are probably the stock of a special train. (Courtesy of Kingfisher Postcards)

Woodstock station, *c*.1910. Pupils and staff of the National School next door had a free return trip to Kidlington on the first train in 1890. (Courtesy of Kingfisher Postcards)

April the chief directors and engineers of the GWR Company 'tested the line' with Mr Lucas, 'travelling in two double carriages attached to an ordinary engine'. Considerable interest was shown on the arrival of the train at the platform of the new station at 1.00 p.m. The visitors afterwards proceeded to the Palace for luncheon'. On 9 May, the Woodstock Railway Company invited the Board of Trade to inspect their line.

Its inspector, Colonel F.H. Rich, RE, surveyed the branch on Wednesday 14 May, travelling over it in a two-coach special train hauled by tank engine number 132, the contractors' locomotive. After stopping to examine the bridges, the inspector's train arrived at Woodstock. But for some minor details, all seemed in order, and Colonel Rich wrote up his report (in two parts – one for the extension and one for the branch proper) in which he recommended that the Board of Trade 'sanction the opening of the new line for passenger traffic'. On the afternoon of Saturday 17 May the GWR made the official announcement the townspeople had been waiting to hear – the Woodstock Railway would open to the public on the following Monday morning.

The Woodstock branch line therefore finally opened for passengers and goods traffic on Monday 19 May 1890, but 'there was no official recognition of the opening on the part of the Corporation', said the *Oxford Times,* putting this down to 'the fact that until the extreme end of last week little or nothing had oozed out' about the event. A train had come down from Oxford earlier in the morning and now formed the first public working out of the terminus at Woodstock. This 'started at 8 am and every carriage was well filled', *Jackson's Oxford Journal* reported, 'a numerous company of the townspeople on the platform cheering lustily as it

The 0-6-0 loco 5413 at Woodstock station, *c.*1950.

steamed out of the attractive little station.' Most of the 120 passengers on it travelled only as far as Kidlington, however.

The train ran on to Oxford, arriving there at 08.26, and those who stayed aboard 'had the great advantage of continuing the journey without changing'. Returning from Oxford at 08.50, it was back in Woodstock by 09.15. On the next train, at 11.05, 'the children and teachers of the National Schools, numbering 214, were treated with a ride to Kidlington', cheering loudly as they departed and returned. The treat was provided through the generosity of gentlemen like Mr Robert Rowles (Mayor) and the Revd A. Majendie (Rector), 'the juveniles thoroughly enjoying the excursion' – and the fact that they had the rest of the day off school! On the opening day, 432 passengers in all travelled on the line, (7 first class, 7 second class and 418 third class).

The Woodstock Railway public service comprised five passenger trains each way each day, except Sundays. All ran through to Oxford bar one, the 18.15 service, which went only to and from Kidlington, (by which name the erstwhile Woodstock Road station was now known). The first and last trains worked empty from and to Oxford, All trains catered for three classes of passengers, at fares of 8d and 1s 8d (first class), 6d and 1s 3d (second class), and 3d and 9d (third class), to Kidlington and Oxford respectively. According to *Jackson's Oxford Journal,* the branch line 'will be a great boon to the inhabitants of the district, and a lasting debt of gratitude is due to the Duke of Marlborough for his munificence in having it constructed'.

Neither the B&CD Railway nor the Woodstock Railway were conceived as progeny of the GWR. One had its origins in the ambitions of a far-sighted millowner while the other owed its creation to the magnanimity of a distinguished landlord. However, within a few years of their opening, both were purchased by the GWR under the terms of the Great Western Railway (Additional Powers) Act of 1897, the former for £138,000 and the latter for £15,000. The Kings Sutton-Chipping Norton section was the final link in a 47-mile-long cross-country route which became one of the longest 'branches' on the GWR. The Kidlington-Woodstock line was a modest affair, less than four miles long, which became an 'archetypal' GWR branch railway.

# 12   Blenheim bound

It may well have been an 'archetypal' GWR branch, but the Kidlington-Woodstock line's terminus station had a special merit. It was located just a short distance from Blenheim Palace, stately home of the Duke of Marlborough, the distinguished landlord who was the line's creator. It was named Blenheim & Woodstock, reflecting its origins in the Victorian era. '[I]n plebian Britain today', the railway historian George Behrend claimed, 'such a station would be called Woodstock (for Blenheim)', with the palace in parentheses. He argued that 'placing a palace first and a large village second' made it a typically Great Western station name. Be that as it may, like the Cherwell Valley line before it, the Woodstock branch was once patronized by some very important people, whose ultimate destination was indeed Blenheim Palace.

The branch terminus was conceived and constructed to receive such passengers. At the date of its opening, the *Oxford Times* called it a 'well-fitted station ... with all the latest improvements, and signalling and other gear sufficient for a place of much larger size'. A typically GWR station building had been erected, but using Cotswold Stone instead of timber. The terminus also possessed a stone-built weigh-house, a corrugated-iron engine shed, a tall wooden signal box and trackwork adequate to cater for special excursion trains of ten coaches or more. Goods sidings gave access to a corrugated-iron goods shed, coal wharves and carriage and cattle docks. In its early years, the terminus dealt with traffic generated by events such as the fire brigades' review of 1895, when trainloads of firemen travelled to Blenheim for military-style parades.

Under the terms of the Woodstock Railway's operating agreement, staff for the branch were supplied by the GWR, including Blenheim & Woodstock's first stationmaster, Mr Albert William Lofting. He had been stationmaster at Kidlington since September 1888 (at an annual salary of £85) but served at Woodstock from its opening until December 1894 (with his annual salary rising from £100 to £110, reflecting his 'promotion'). The GWR also supplied the branch with rolling stock and locomotives, the latter usually being number 1473 (a 517-class 0-4-2 tank engine built in 1883). It was named *Fair Rosamund* early in 1896 in memory of Rosamund Clifford, King Henry II's mistress at Woodstock. The naming was possibly intended to raise the status of an otherwise ordinary engine and so impress important passengers on the branch.

Certainly, the branch engine was named in a year when some very important people were Blenheim bound. The 8th Duke of Marlborough, who promoted the Woodstock Railway, had died in 1892, being succeeded by his son as the 9th Duke. Like his father, the son married a wealthy American heiress, in this case Miss Consuelo Vanderbilt (based on finance rather than romance, it was an unhappy union which eventually ended in divorce). The couple were wed in November

*Fair Rosamund* at Woodstock station in 1906, with the Woodstock Corps of the St John Ambulance Brigade posing on the platform. (Courtesy of Mrs R. Giraud)

1895 at the Episcopal Church of St Thomas, Fifth Avenue, New York. Following a prolonged wedding tour abroad, the couple did not return to England until March 1896. They spent two days at a London hotel before starting their journey to Oxfordshire, where reception committees had been busy making arrangements to welcome home the newly-weds.

The Duke and Duchess travelled down from London on Tuesday 31 March, in a special saloon carriage attached to the rear of the 13.30 Paddington-Birkenhead express, which pulled into Oxford station at 14.48. Such a large crowd of sightseers from the neighbourhood had assembled to greet the couple that part of the platform had been roped off to prevent crushing. The GWR official in charge of the railway arrangements was Mr Edward Murphy (the Birmingham District Superintendent), who was waiting with Mr Gibbs (the Reading Divisional Superintendent) and Mr Davis (the Oxford stationmaster) to welcome the couple. The Duke and Duchess stood at the saloon door and 'appeared highly satisfied with the hearty reception'. Meanwhile, their saloon was uncoupled from the express which then continued on its way to Birkenhead.

Next, the Woodstock branch engine, *Fair Rosamund*, decorated with evergreens, the Stars and Stripes and the words 'Welcome Home' at the front, backed onto the saloon to complete the journey to Woodstock. At precisely three o'clock, the special train set off, to the accompaniment of hearty cheers from the spectators and a *feu de joie* of detonators placed on the rails over which it ran. Groups of well-wishers waited at locations such as Walton Well Bridge and Wolvercote Junction to catch a glimpse of the distinguished travellers and cheer them on their way. At Kidlington – the junction from the main line to the branch – a brief stop was made and 'their Graces met with the first of the many pleasant experiences which

An early photograph (almost certainly pre-First World War) of *Fair Rosamund* at Woodstock. (Courtesy of Mrs R. Giraud)

A unique photograph of a steam railmotor at Woodstock. The picture is undated. (Courtesy of Mrs R. Giraud)

*Fair Rosamund* at Woodstock with her crew in the 1920s. On the right is the branch train guard, Tommy Hine. (Courtesy of Mrs R. Giraud)

Woodstock Station, *c.*1950. Following the closure of the branch line in 1954, the station building became Young's garage. (Courtesy of R.H.G. Simpson)

befell them during the afternoon'. The village's railway station had been transformed for the occasion.

The down platform, at which the special train stopped, had been 'artistically decorated'. A mass of foliage, relieved with cut flowers, hid the gas standards from view, while the spaces between them were filled with flowering azaleas, arum lilies, ferns and other pot plants sent from Aynho rectory and a Mr Arnall of Oxford. A number of flags 'lent colour and variety' and to complete the effect a 'floral device representing the letters 'M' or 'V'' was fixed to each lamp standard. On the road bridge at the end of the platform, evergreens were fixed around the arch and the word 'Welcome' was picked out in red japonica. These floral decorations had been put in place under the direction of the Kidlington stationmaster, Mr William Thomas Cooke, (who had succeeded Mr Lofting here in 1890 and stayed for thirty-seven years until he retired in May 1927).

Mr Cooke's younger daughter, Winifred, presented a bouquet of roses to the Duchess, who 'expressed her delight at the appearance of the station'. His elder daughter, Florence, on behalf of her father, presented a handsome red morocco case designed for holding a timetable card for local trains to the Duke, who 'expressed his gratification with the gift'. Mr Cooke declared that he 'should be pleased to supply his Grace with timetable cards every month'. After a short wait, the special train steamed away, Blenheim-bound, to the cheers of villagers gathered near the platform and on the road overbridge. As it sped onwards, 'little knots of spectators clustered around the farmhouses' and flags 'caught the eye from time to time in the trees and meadows' alongside the railway, telling the Duchess 'that she was at last nearing home'.

At Woodstock station too a transformation had taken place. The platform was divided down the middle and carpeted, and the station wall was hung with bullion-fringed red baize. The booking hall was curtained off and converted into a reception room, being tastefully furnished with palms, arum lilies and other pot plants. Here, floral decoration had been effected under the control of Mr Thomas Ashford, (who had succeeded Mr Lofting as Blenheim & Woodstock stationmaster in 1894). People with the necessary passes waited on the arrival platform while pupils of the National School massed on the opposite platform. Thousands more congregated in the roadway outside the station. A bell rang in the stationmaster's office to announce that the train was on its way and at 15.18 it arrived in the station to the cheers of the assembled multitude.

The Duke and Duchess made their way to the booking hall and emerged 'evidently gratified and surprised at their hearty reception'. They were escorted to their carriage outside the station, where the Duke raised his hat to the cheering crowds as they were driven away to celebrations at Woodstock Town Hall and ultimately at Blenheim Palace itself, where the day ended in a spectacular firework display. The people of Oxfordshire were present throughout on the day and a considerable number of them travelled to and from Blenheim by train – the total number of passengers booking from Oxford was put at about 1,300. Train services between Oxford and Woodstock were duplicated during both morning and afternoon, with two extra outward services and three extra return services in addition to the normal train service on the branch.

After this special day in the spring, more important people were Blenheim bound in the autumn of the same year when the Prince and Princess of Wales made another pre-Christmas visit to Blenheim. They had not done so for over twenty years following the quarrel between the Prince and the Marlboroughs in 1875, but the deaths of the 8th Duke (in 1892) and Lord Randolph Churchill (in 1895) cleared the way for a visit to be made in 1896. So it was that Edward and Alexandra (with their daughter, Princess Victoria) came to visit the 9th Duke and his new wife at Blenheim Palace. Previously, their train journey from London had ended at Kidlington (or 'Woodstock Road' as it was then) as the most convenient railhead, but the opening of the Woodstock branch now allowed them to travel almost to the gates of the palace by rail.

Their royal train left Paddington at 16.55 on Monday 23 November in the charge of GWR official Mr T.I. Allen, the Superintendent of the line. The train consisted of a main line locomotive at the front, a six-wheeled brake van, a saloon carriage for the royal party, two more saloons for the rest of the visitors and an eight-wheeled brake van at the rear. It ran non-stop to Kidlington station – decorated as it had been in the spring – where a change of locomotives was effected, and *Fair Rosamund* took it onwards over the branch. The little branch engine 'wore an aspect less unlovely than usual, being gaily decked for the occasion'. The word 'Welcome' surrounded by a large wreath of fir leaves was mounted on its front while several small flags (including the Stars and Stripes and the Union flag) were placed in prominent positions.

Blenheim & Woodstock station had again been transformed. The open part of the platform was screened with a temporary structure 156 feet in length, so that on its arrival the whole of the royal train would be flanked by a draped and brilliantly illuminated corridor, 'the cosiness of which was in striking contrast to the bare and draughty platform a few hours previously'. The platform was carpeted and decorated for a distance of 212 feet, and the whole wall was covered in crimson baize with a fringe of amber material. To relieve the wall covering, large palms were placed at intervals along the platform, with framed views of GWR holiday resorts between them. The roof was lined with red, white and green striped bunting and lit by suspended lamps and others on brackets. The words 'Welcome' and 'Come Again' were displayed on the station walls.

Overall control of the arrangements at the station was in the hands of the GWR General Manager, Mr J.L. Wilkinson, assisted by Mr W.C. Simpson of Paddington and Mr Ashford, the stationmaster. The decoration was carried out by local staff and up to the last minute 'the servants were busy with their preparations, and every speck of dust was scrupulously swept from the carpet over which the Royal and distinguished visitors were to walk on alighting from the train'. As the arrival time drew nigh, only a privileged few were allowed into the station precincts, including the GWR's Birmingham Division Superintendent, Mr Edward Murphy, who had control of the line from Kidlington to Woodstock. The Duke of Marlborough arrived at the station in a carriage just before 18.30 and entered the specially decorated waiting room to await the train.

A bell rang in the stationmaster's office to announce that the royal train was on its way along the branch and at 18.39 (a minute early) it 'steamed slowly and almost noiselessly into the station, the pennons with which the engine was adorned floating gaily in the breeze'. As the Prince and Princess alighted from their saloon the Duke stepped forward to greet them and it was observed that 'their Royal Highnesses were looking in the best of health'. The royal party proceeded through a reception area in the booking hall, where a corridor of baize and other hangings had been constructed and which was furnished with chrysanthemums and foliage plants supplied by Mr Whillans, the Duke's head gardener. They then passed out into the street from where they were conveyed in the Duke's carriage – an open landau – to Blenheim Palace itself.

'Never before in the history of the Borough of Woodstock has the quaint little town been seen under more brilliant and joyous conditions', declared the *Oxford Times* in its report of the visit. Certainly, the GWR was 'bent on giving a hearty welcome to the Duke's royal and other distinguished visitors', and their decorations at Blenheim & Woodstock station were as lavish as those that had been provided at Oxford station on Sunday 4 October when the Tsar of Russia visited the city en route from Balmoral to Portsmouth (bound for France). Moreover, the GWR General Manager, Mr Wilkinson, had taken a personal interest in the arrangements and given explicit instructions to his staff to do 'everything possible to please the Duke and to give the Prince a hearty reception'. The GWR also ran extra trains to and from Woodstock on the day.

However, the *Oxford Times* noted that compared with the multitude which lined the streets of Woodstock for the return of the Duke and Duchess in the spring, 'the number of spectators on the present occasion was considerably smaller'. It was true that the town's streets were lined on either side with inhabitants of the town and visitors from the district but 'there was no crushing except in the immediate vicinity of the station where, as might be anticipated, the crowd was most dense'. As in the spring, the town was yet again decorated, with flags, floral arches and hundreds of fairy lights strung out along the road from the railway station to the town hall. The reasons for the smaller crowds may have included the autumnal weather, rumours of the 1875 quarrel or perhaps simply that the novelty of VIP visits was losing its appeal!

The royal party stayed at Blenheim Palace until the end of the week. On the Monday evening, the procession from the station to the palace was followed by a grand dinner. The next two days were spent shooting rabbits in Blenheim Park and pheasants at North Leigh Coverts respectively. Thursday morning was spent rabbit shooting and was followed by an afternoon visit to Oxford (by road). That evening, there was an illuminated cycle parade, torchlight procession, bonfire and firework display at Blenheim. Thousands of visitors flocked to the event by road and rail: no fewer than 3,217 passengers were booked from Oxford and the GWR found it necessary to run extra trains in addition to the ordinary branch service.

There were five heavily laden specials outbound and seven back, the first arriving in Oxford at 23.40 and the last at about 02.25.

On the Friday, rabbit shooting at Bladon was followed by a reception at Blenheim Palace in the evening. Next day – Saturday 28 November – the royal party left for the Prince's residence at Sandringham. Edward and Alexandra, with their daughter, set out from the palace at 10.00, first travelling to Oxford by road with an escort of Yeomanry cavalry. The rest of the royal entourage left from Blenheim & Woodstock station at 10.45 on a special train to Oxford's GWR station. Here the Prince of Wales, with his wife and daughter, joined them to continue their journey on to Norfolk via the LNWR line through Bletchley. Thus ended the first such royal visit in over twenty years, but it began a period, lasting through and beyond Edward's reign, in which special trains – for people who were Blenheim bound – often travelled on the Woodstock branch.

On the occasion of his pre-Christmas visit in 1899, the Prince of Wales brought a guest with him – the Kaiser of Germany! Kaiser Wilhelm, with his wife and two sons, arrived in England on 20 November, coming ashore at the Southern Railway jetty, Portsmouth, and travelling by rail to stay with his English cousins at Windsor Castle. It seems that last-minute plans were made to include in the itinerary a flying visit of a 'purely private' nature to Blenheim, and this took place on Friday 24 November 1899. The Kaiser – without his own family but accompanied by the Prince of Wales and the Duke of Connaught – travelled on a special train consisting of three of the Queen's royal saloons with a guard's van at each end. This special train left the GWR's Windsor branch at 12 noon and joined the main line at Slough for its journey to Woodstock.

The Great Western's working timetable stipulated that the royal train should run ahead of the 11.45 express from Paddington and pass through the 'middle road' at Oxford without stopping. Three minutes were allowed for an engine change at Kidlington, where the main line engine was uncoupled (and ran light to Oxford to be turned) while the branch engine coupled up to take the train onwards. It 'reached Woodstock punctually at a quarter past one o'clock'. Waiting at the station were the Duke and Duchess of Marlborough, Lord and Lady Curzon, and Lord Valentia, MP, and 'on the stoppage of the train the Emperor, the Prince of Wales, and the Duke of Connaught alighted and cordially shook hands with their graces'. They were also received by the Mayor (Mr John Banbury) and the corporation, although no official reception had been arranged.

The Woodstock Troop of the Queen's Own Oxfordshire Hussars formed a guard of honour as the party left the station. They entered an open carriage to drive into the town and through the park gate, where more guards of honour waited, composed of firemen (the Duke of Marlborough was the Chairman of the Fire Brigades' Union). Luncheon was followed by a drive around the park and before leaving the Kaiser planted a conifer to commemorate his visit, which was

*Opposite*: A GWR working notice issued to employees before the visit of Kaiser Wilhelm in 1899.

(No 240.)

# GREAT WESTERN RAILWAY.

(For the use of the Company's Servants only.)

## NOTICE OF

# SPECIAL TRAIN

FROM

# *WINDSOR*

TO

# *BLENHEIM*

**AND BACK,**

ON

# Friday, November 24th, 1899.

## TIME TABLE.

| FORWARD JOURNEY. | | arr. P.M. | pass dep. NOON | RETURN JOURNEY. | arr. P.M. | pass dep. P.M. | |
|---|---|---|---|---|---|---|---|
| **WINDSOR** ... ... | | — | 12 0 | **BLENHEIM** ... ... | | | Time of return uncertain. |
| Slough West Curve | **A** | ML 12 6 | | Kidlington ... ... | | | Special will probably leave **Blenheim about 3.30** p.m. |
| Maidenhead ... ... | | | 12 12 | Oxford (Middle Road) | | | |
| Reading ... ... | | | 12 24 | Didcot East Junction | | | |
| Didcot East Junction | | | 12 43 | Reading ... ... | | | Station Masters at all Stations must be on the look out for telegraphic advice and must endeavour to keep a clear road for the Special. |
| Oxford (Middle Road) | | | 12 56 | Maidenhead ... ... | | | |
| Kidlington ... ... | **B** | 1 4 | 1 7 | Slough West Curve ... | | | |
| **BLENHEIM** ... ... | | 1 15 | — | **WINDSOR** ... ... | | | |

 **A** To precede the 11.45 a.m. Express from Paddington from Slough.

 **B** A Separate Engine to be provided at Kidlington on Down journey to enable Train Engine to be detached there and run to Oxford to turn. Train Engine to return to Blenheim in good time to work the Special Train through from there to Windsor.

marked by fine weather, the day being cold but clear. The royal visitors 'left the Palace at about half-past four o'clock' for the short drive to the station where 'the assembled crowd' gave them 'a hearty send-off'. The GWR working timetable stated 'Time of return uncertain', adding that the 'Special will probably leave Blenheim about 3.30 p.m.' In fact it departed an hour later.

Having turned at Oxford, the train engine had reversed down to Blenheim and was ready to work the special through from there to Windsor. Staff at all the stations *en route* had been warned to 'look out for telegraphic advice' and to 'keep a clear road for the special' on its journey, to ensure the prompt return of the visitors to Windsor Castle that evening. The Imperial visit to Queen Victoria ended next day, when the Kaiser and his family travelled to Sandringham, staying as guests of the Prince and Princess of Wales. On 28 November they travelled by rail to Sheerness, from where they embarked for Germany. More distinguished visitors found themselves Blenheim bound as the nineteenth century gave way to the twentieth, but the Woodstock townsfolk would not have reason to make the Kaiser welcome again in the years after 1899!

# 13    Further afield

Apart from branch lines, railway development around the turn of the century consisted of the construction of the country's last trunk lines and many connecting links, or 'cut-offs'. Britain's total route mileage increased from 20,073 in 1890 to 23,441 in 1912; although this was not a dramatic growth in the railway network many of the extensions were of vital importance in an age when there were still few other viable forms of transport. The GWR was actively involved in two new railway schemes – one a trunk route and the other a 'cut off' – both of which came into contact with its Cherwell Valley line in the vicinity of Banbury.

One of them was Britain's last main line, the Great Central Railway, formed when the Manchester, Sheffield & Lincolnshire Railway was united with the Metropolitan Railway. The GCR was the brainchild of Sir Edward Watkin who conceived it as a rail link from the North of England to France via London and a Channel Tunnel. This ambitious dream came to nought but a Great Central 'extension' line from Annesley (near Nottingham) via Leicester and Rugby to Quainton Road (near Aylesbury), thus giving access to a terminus at Marylebone station in London, did get built. It opened for public passenger services on 15 March 1899.

By this date, the GWR and GCR had already formed an alliance to create a short connecting link between their main lines which would open up a new route from the north and east to the south and west. The GWR had persuaded the GCR to make the link from its new main line near Woodford Halse to the Cherwell Valley line at Banbury. Such was the potential of the link (authorised in 1897) that the GWR was granted powers to build it should the GCR fail to do so. The Great Western agreed to lend its ally the necessary capital and did in fact finance the work, although it was carried out by a contractor appointed by the Great Central.

Construction was undertaken by Messrs Walter Scott & Company of Newcastle and Westminster, who were contractors for the GCR between Charwelton and Quainton Road as well as on the link line to Banbury. Their agent was Mr T. Middleton with Mr Colin Smith as resident engineer. Capital of £200,000 was authorised for construction of the link, which entailed the excavation of a total of 1,500,000 cubic tons of spoil from its $8\frac{1}{2}$ mile length. Some 800 men were engaged in building the line, assisted by six steam navvies, of which four were employed in digging a $1\frac{1}{2}$ mile-long cutting at Thorpe Mandeville.

The line left the GCR extension at Culworth from a new junction, the construction of which caused problems for the contractors. In his autobiography, countryman Syd Tyrrell (1889-1976) of Eydon recalled talk of a bed of 'running sand' that made embankments unstable. The branch line bank 'slipped away' from the main line bank several times: 'Making up had to be done, for it was some time before the two consolidated to form a stable union'. Local sand and gravel was used in building work wherever it was available. For instance, 'a pit was opened in the fields between Eydon and Culworth' for its extraction.

Thorpe Mandeville cutting was the heaviest engineering task on the route. 'It gave the contractors a great deal of trouble, owing to the position of the rock beds, and for blasting purposes no less than twelve tons of tonite [*sic*]were used'. In all, 900,000 cubic yards of spoil was removed, to a width of 280 feet from the top of one slope to the other, and a depth of 50 feet for a distance of half a mile. Here was the line's steepest gradient – 1 in 132 – by which means the railway dropped 150 feet from the hills. Most of the spoil was taken out at the south end and used in building a three-mile-long embankment across Chacombe Meadows.

The other gradients were easier although another deep cutting was made near Culworth, this time through clay. The spoil from this was used to build an embankment between the cutting and a bridge at the fork in the road from Culworth to Eydon and Edgecote. At the behest of Brackley Rural District Council, a close-boarded fence was erected on the bridge and trees were planted on the bank to screen the trains from passing horses. Double tracks of 86lb rails were laid and joined to the GWR main line at Banbury Junction, where exchange sidings for freight were set out and a signal box built 'with all the latest appliances'.

When the junction at Banbury had been inspected and approved, coal and other freight trains began to run over the new line from 1 June 1900, helping the earthworks to settle prior to running passenger trains over it. On 22 June the connection was used by a special cattle train from the West of England on its way northward to York, where the Royal Show was being held during that week. The Board of Trade inspection of the line was conducted on Thursday 28 June by Colonel Von Donop, who travelled along the new railway from Culworth Junction on the GCR to Banbury Junction on the GWR and made the usual checks.

The seventy-five new bridges were subjected to particular scrutiny. All of them were found satisfactory: 'the greatest deflection of any girder was a quarter of an inch'. The bridge across the Daventry Road contained seventy tons of steelwork, while the road bridge over Thorpe Mandeville cutting, with three arches each of 55ft 6in span, contained 2,417 cubic yards of brickwork. The signal boxes and 'lay-by' sidings at Chacombe and Culworth were also examined. In the inspection, everything 'proved of the most satisfactory character', so the line was duly declared fit for passenger traffic and opened on Monday 13 August 1900.

The alliance between the GWR and the GCR immediately resulted in a valuable new through rail link, potentially 'among the most important of any not touching the metropolis'. A weekday express service of two trains each way was inaugurated between Leicester and Oxford but these long-distance trains did not stop at Banbury, a fact soon taken up in a letter written to the local newspaper: 'I have been waiting for weeks to go by that line to Leicester. I trust that the town

The 13.50 'Little Banbury' to Woodford (on the ex-GCR main line) at Banbury station, 25 August 1965. The loco is the ex-LNER tank engine number 67789. (Courtesy of Michael Mensing)

council will not let the Company rest before they ask them to have a train stop at Banbury'. It was signed by 'A disappointed one'.

The following week it was reported that Mr G.E. Heydon, of the Public Boot Supply Company in Parsons Street, had written to the GWR with reference to the non-stopping of Oxford-Leicester trains at Banbury station and 'had received a reply to the effect that the matter is receiving attention'. By the autumn, the two express trains were indeed stopping at Banbury! On and from 1 December 1900 the weekday through service increased to five trains each way, extended south to Bournemouth (four ex-Manchester, one ex-York), and north to Manchester (two ex-Bournemouth, two ex-Portsmouth, one ex-Reading).

At the date of the opening the branch service consisted of three daily shuttle trains each way. At this time there were no intermediate stations on the line, which ran through grazing country populated only by farming villages. However, two platform halts were built later: Chacombe Road (opened on 17 April 1911) and Eydon Road (opened on 1 October 1913), which also served Thorpe Mandeville and Culworth, being closer to the latter village than the station of that name on the GCR main line. By then, the 'Little Banbury', a tank engine and two coaches, made five daily trips along the branch 'with clockwork regularity'.

For the men working in the fields, the passing trains were 'a never-failing source of interest' and 'useful to tell the time, as few of them carried watches', Syd

Tyrrell recalled. 'Another boon the railway brought', he says, 'was the national newspapers on the day of publication' – the railway was opened during the Boer War and, with local men in the fighting forces, the villagers were keen to hear the latest. Even on the GCR main line at Culworth Junction, the signal box was surrounded by open countryside, which 'belied its importance' as it was 'deafeningly quiet except when the birds' song was broken by the sound of a train'.

Woodford, once a sleepy village, soon developed into a railway community centred on its locomotive depot, marshalling yards and junction station, named 'Woodford and Hinton'. (It became 'Woodford Halse' in 1948.) The station served the parish of Woodford-cum-Membris, comprising the villages of Woodford Halse, Hinton and West Farndon. The last two were separated by the River Cherwell, which has its source near Charwelton, the next station north, at the summit level of the GCR extension. Thus the new line created a rail connection from the stripling Cherwell above Woodford to the mature river below Banbury.

The little section of line between Banbury and Woodford was responsible for a huge increase in freight traffic on the GCR, most of which found its way onto the GWR. 'The new line is one of great importance for the access it gives to the north and vice versa', commented the *Banbury Guardian* on its opening. 'A glance at the map shows that it is almost a straight line from the Annesley coalfields to Winchester, Southampton and Portsmouth, so that a large amount of mineral and goods traffic may be anticipated to those parts as well as to Bristol and the West'. There was also fish from Grimsby for Plymouth and South Wales.

In the meantime, the Great Central Railway and the Metropolitan – its erstwhile ally – had quarrelled, with the result that the former experienced difficulty in working its trains into London via Aylesbury. Consequently, the GCR sought an alternative route into Marylebone, being aided and abetted by the GWR – its new ally – which wished to construct a more direct line from Paddington to Birmingham. In 1899 a GW & GC Railways Joint Line Committee was formed to share the task of bringing this about by building a new and improved railway between Acton and Aynho via High Wycombe. It became the last main line built in England.

The southern section, shared by the GWR and GCR, was completed first and the latter's passenger trains began using it from April 1906, running to and from their own main line on a link between Ashendon (GWR) and Grendon Underwood (GCR) junctions. The northern section was not ready for four more years. Designed by the GWR engineer, Mr William Armstrong, it was 18 miles 29 chains in length and ran from Ashendon to Aynho. Here, a new 'flying junction' was constructed to link it to the Cherwell Valley line. The contractors were Messrs Scott and Middleton of Westminster, with Mr R.C. Sikes as resident engineer.

In building this section, the contractors excavated 2,700,000 cubic yards of clay and rock, most of which was used in making the embankments. They had to build

The 2-8-0 locomotive 2836 at Aynho Junction on 29 August 1962 with a down freight train. The Bicester cut-off joins the Cherwell Valley main line here, passing over a flyover and around the back of the signal box on its down route. (Courtesy of Michael Mensing)

twelve overbridges and seven underbridges (eleven of girderwork, seven of brick and one of mixed brick and girder). At Ardley, a tunnel 1,147yds long and 100ft below the surface of the ground was dug in just eighteen months. At Aynho, two viaducts were erected, each over 50ft high with brick piers and arches and 40ft spans – one was of eighteen spans, the other of twenty-four. The construction involved some 'very heavy' work but the contractors 'completed their work without serious hindrance'.

The permanent way was finished in the spring of 1910 and although there was no formal ceremony the laying of the last rail was a matter of note. It took place on the afternoon of Tuesday 29 March at a point 30 yards north of the signal box at Aynho Junction, on the near side of the up line. Shortly after two o'clock, a gang of workmen carried the last rail to the spot and lowered it onto its chairs; 'a twist with some crowbars sent it with a clink into its place'. Fishplates were bolted on to connect it to the adjoining rails, and 'at twenty minutes past two o'clock to the minute, Banbury was linked up by its new route to London'.

The job was not yet quite complete, as the length of line still 'presented a somewhat serpentine appearance'. The 200 yards of snaking track next had to be centred on the wooden pegs which had already been laid by the engineers. This task was accomplished by a gang of ten men with crowbars, under a foreman with a tape. The foreman measured the distance from the peg to the rails and gave orders to the gang, who 'leant on their crowbars and the section of metals, sleepers and all, moved bodily on the permanent way'. Another gang of men followed, throwing on ballast so the line 'was to all intents and purposes complete'.

At the end of that week the contractor's men left the site and the GWR took over the line as a going concern. It was opened for goods trains on 4 April 1910 and for passenger trains on 1 July. There were stations at Brill & Ludgershall, Blackthorn, Bicester, Ardley and Aynho Park Platform on the new section, which joined the old line to Banbury just beyond the existing Aynho station. This 'Bicester Cut-off' reduced the distance from Paddington to Birmingham via Oxford by almost nineteen miles, with corresponding savings in journey times. The new Great Western route to Birmingham was two miles shorter than the LNWR's.

The opening day was a Friday, and the GWR laid on a special train for the initial passenger service, offering a return journey to London for 'a large party representing commerce and other interests in Birmingham and elsewhere'. The Lord Mayor of Birmingham, with other members of the Corporation, travelled by the new route to the capital, where a reception was held at the Grand Hotel. Prior to the opening, the GWR had improved the permanent way along the entire distance between London and Birmingham by 'laying down heavier lines on a slag ballast foundation', so affording passengers a more comfortable ride.

The Great Western station at Bicester, with the first express train on the Bicester cut-off passing through on 1 July 1910, taking passengers from Paddington to Birmingham in just two hours. (Courtesy of Kingfisher Postcards)

At Banbury, there were forty-six passengers for London and various stations on the new line on the opening day. The first service available to them was a five coach train, 'four of them being the most modern and largest carriages'. These were hauled by locomotive number 4104, named *Auricula* (the first of twenty 4-4-0 locomotives of the 'Flower' class, built in 1908). The train carried only four first class and just twenty-four third class passengers but, as a local newspaper commented, 'it is well known that railway travellers are slow to change their habits' and 'those who once try the new line will not desire the old (with the endless wait at Oxford) again in a hurry'.

The train left Banbury at 10.30 'along the familiar Cherwell Vale' and was soon at Aynho Junction, where it set out on the new line. Considerable care was taken by the driver in crossing the embankment between the Aynho viaducts and Ardley tunnel on account of the newness of the earthworks, but 'a good pace was again resumed' beyond it as the train entered a two-mile-long rock cutting. Bicester (fourteen miles from Banbury) was passed at 10.46 and Ashendon Junction at 10.55. The train arrived at High Wycombe station at 11.17 and, after pausing briefly, departed for Paddington, arriving in the terminus at 11.44 (a minute early).

This train was one of four offering Banbury fast through services to and from London. Trains were timetabled to depart at 10.27 and 12.10 in the up direction, arriving in the capital at 11.45 and 13.25. From Paddington, passengers left on trains at 14.35 and 16.00, reaching Banbury at 15.47 and 15.13, and arrived in the town on the first train in a slip coach released from its rear as it passed through non-stop! This train replaced what had previously been the town's sole non-stop service, which had left Paddington at 14.15 and travelled via Oxford to slip a coach at Banbury at 15.46. The other three trains were brand new services.

Journey time between Banbury and London were cut to 1 hour 15 minutes up and 1 hour 12 minutes down, saving around twenty minutes on these fast trains. Only three other daily expresses on the new route did not stop or slip a coach at Banbury. There were further trains between the town and the capital but they were slower and were intended to open up the intervening countryside, the GWR using them 'to develop and serve the districts through which it runs'. A local shuttle service of 'auto-trains' – one or two carriages, usually coupled to a 517 class 0-4-2 tank engine – ran back and forth from Banbury to Bicester (and beyond).

Commenting on the opening of the Bicester cut-off, the *Banbury Guardian* concluded that 'the new service is altogether a substantial addition to the railway accommodation of Banbury' As a result, the town was now 'unrivalled in its railway facilities'. Moreover, although the timetable for the old line via Oxford was revised, the number of trains by this route was largely unchanged. Over the 'northern line' as a whole, the GWR had already effected several improvements to the timetable, so that what had once been regarded as a generally slow service was 'revised and smartened up' all the way between London and Birkenhead.

The GWR's first corridor train had been built in 1891 and had made its debut on the 13.30 service from Paddington to Birkenhead on 7 March 1892.

Gangwayed throughout and heated by steam, it had lavatory accommodation for all three classes! The Midland Railway had abolished second class and upgraded third class to this level as early as 1874, an example soon followed by other companies, but on the Great Western the final abolition of second class carriages coincided with the opening of the Bicester cut-off. By July 1910 trains on the northern line consisted of corridor coaches, with refreshments served on almost all of them.

The GWR had done little to attract passengers from the LNWR until well after the abolition of the broad gauge in 1869, at which point Great Western trains took up to four hours to cover its longer route between London and Birmingham. A new fast train from Paddington had entered service in June, 1880, reaching Birmingham in 2 hours 42 minutes. The first train to pass Oxford non-stop was a London-North Wales express put on in July 1892, which reached Leamington (106 miles) in two hours. This same train became the first to run non-stop as far as Birmingham in 2 hours 27 minutes during the summer-only service of July 1898. From 1899 a permanent down service, the 14.10 ex-Paddington, commenced a regular non-stop service to Birmingham in 2 hours 25 minutes. A further speed-up was effected from July, 1902, when one up and three down services completed the 129 mile journey in 2 hours 20 minutes, at an average speed of 55.3 miles per hour. The LNWR began operating a 2-hour service between Euston and Birmingham, by its shorter route, in 1905 but it was not until the GWR opened the Bicester cut-off in 1910 – and reduced the distance its trains had to travel – that it was able to introduce its own 2-hour express service from Paddington.

When the northern line expresses were diverted to the new route from 1 July 1910, the Great Western was able to provide an even two-hour service between London and Birmingham. As the cut-off line was nearly nineteen miles shorter than the old route via Oxford, the twenty minutes saved on the journey time did not involve any real increase in speed, although the gradients were much steeper. However, by substituting for its circuitous Cherwell Valley line a more direct 'cut-off' route – as elsewhere on its straggling system – the GWR was at last able to shake off the epithet of 'Great Way Round' by which it had been known.

# 14   Conflict and casualties

The early twentieth century was a period of considerable activity in both national life and rail travel. At the beginning of 1901 Queen Victoria died and on 2 February a funeral train took her body from Paddington to Windsor. Elsewhere on the GWR, more trains than ever entered service. In 1902 a new train was put on between Swindon and Leicester via the GCR as well as a new buffet car express between York and Oxford (with through coaches to Bournemouth). In 1903, the GCR timetable showed four trains each way daily between Sheffield and Bournemouth via Oxford and also a morning Bristol-Nottingham service. From May 1906 the new through line at Kingham was used by a cross-country service inaugurated between Newcastle and Barry with one train each way daily (except Sundays) via Woodford, Banbury and the B&CDR.

By 1910 the service via Oxford and the GCR had increased to seven down and six up trains to Nottingham and beyond. At the same date, the GWR's Bicester cut-off resulted in extra trains between London and Birmingham via Banbury, in addition to the existing main and branch line services in the Cherwell Valley. In that year, too, King Edward VII – who had been nearly sixty years old when he succeeded to the throne – died. His funeral train made the same journey as his mother's and was notable for carrying more reigning monarchs than have ever been carried in one train, before or since. When his son, recently crowned as King George V, returned from his coronation durbar to India in 1912, Britain's railways were at their peak. The total number of passenger journeys had grown from 336.5 million in 1870 to 1,294 million in 1912.

However, national developments were soon eclipsed by international events, with the declaration of war between Britain and Germany on 4 August 1914. Next day the British Government took over all the country's railways, vesting their control in a Railway Executive Committee. On the GWR, 632 special troop trains were run during the fortnight of mobilization (including 186 to bring the Territorials from their summer training camps), as well as 190 goods trains carrying military supplies. In spite of all this extra traffic, the ordinary services were fully maintained and only excursion trains were temporarily curtailed. By the end of the first month, 2,470 specials had been run on the Great Western, with 376,787 officers and men, 33,101 horses and 355 guns and limbers despatched from its stations – and many more by other companies.

In the Cherwell Valley, a battalion of the Oxford & Bucks Light Infantry was swiftly mobilized. On Wednesday 5 August 200 soldiers were despatched from Banbury, comprising the men of C and G companies (115 and 85 respectively). They began to assemble at the Drill Hall in Crouch Street from 07.00 and at 10.20 'sombre crowds' lined the route as they marched to the GWR station, where they were given a 'warm reception' by a force of Territorials whose train had stopped

Deddington, seen here in around 1900, was one of many Oxfordshire villages from which troops arrived in Oxford on 5 August 1914. The men entrained at the GWR's nearby Aynho station. (Courtesy of Kingfisher Postcards)

Oxford station. This view is looking west in August 1964. The S.R. Pacific locomotive 34085 *501 Squadron* is waiting to take an express to the South Coast. (Courtesy of David Canning)

there. The Banbury squadron had to wait on the forecourt until the Territorials' train left but they were then allowed onto the up main platform, where their own train pulled in from the sidings. They entrained 'amid great handshaking, the waving of hats, and cheering'. Platform ticket sales were such that the GWR must have 'reaped a considerable harvest from the toll levied'.

The railway arrangements were the responsibility of the Banbury stationmaster, Mr Short, and 'so great was the desire to see the men off' that he clearly had his hands full. Nevertheless, his duties were carried out in a 'most commendable' manner and the soldiers were boarded with 'the utmost despatch'. Their train steamed away and, after calling at Aynho to pick up a detachment of thirty-seven men from Deddington, arrived at Oxford just before noon. Large crowds gathered to watch them march from the station up New Road, Queen Street and down St. Aldate's to Christchurch. The Banbury detachment was joined by contingents from Bicester, Witney, Chipping Norton and Woodstock, all the soldiers being quartered in the city's colleges, many of which were 'thrown open for the use of the military' for the first time since the Civil War 300 years earlier.

Mobilization of the 4th Oxford & Bucks Light Infantry, commanded by Lieutenant-Colonel A. Stockton, was completed without a hitch and by that weekend it was fully equipped and at full strength, with a thousand men. On the evening of Sunday 9 August the battalion left the city. The men were 'in high spirits' and their departure was marked by the 'enthusiasm of the crowd which filled the streets leading to the station'. The battalion was divided for an overnight journey in two trains, one leaving at 21.00 and the other at 23.00. The GWR station and its precincts were crowded, and as the trains steamed away into the night the men were given a memorable send-off, 'the cheering being distinctly heard at the battalion headquarters in St. Cross Road, right on the other side of the city'. It was a rousing departure for Oxfordshire's soldiers.

The destination of the battalion on its departure from Oxford was not made public knowledge at the time for security reasons. In fact, the men appear to have been sent first to Swindon, thence to Leighton Buzzard and Dunstable for training. During the following week – on Tuesday 11 August – the Banbury squadron of the (mounted) Queen's Own Hussars left the town, again travelling by rail from the GWR station. The station approach was kept clear until the horses had been boxed 'and this work was smartly accomplished in about half an hour'. Their train departed at about 11.30 to 'ringing cheers'. Thus, like the nation's other railways, the Cherwell Valley line of the GWR played its part in transporting troops and supplies in the early days of the war. Sadly, the enthusiasm of the soldiers and the euphoria of the crowds did not last long.

Within weeks of the Expeditionary Force's departure, stalemate set in on the Western Front. Casualties began to mount and a steady stream of wounded had to make the journey home. From the field hospitals the troops were taken back to base hospitals and, after treatment, brought back across the Channel on hospital ships to Southampton. They were then conveyed on hospital trains to military hospitals safe inland, manned by the Royal Army Medical Corps. At Swindon, sixteen hospital trains were constructed in all and 238 GWR carriages served as ambulance coaches in the course of the war, some conversions and others specially built. Each ambulance train comprised nine vehicles, with berths for sitting and stretcher wounded cases, day and sleeping accommodation for medical staff, kitchen and dining facilities, and a pharmacy.

Convoys of hospital trains made their way up the Cherwell Valley railway, *en route* from Southampton to the various military hospitals of the midlands and the north. Along all the rail routes there were 'rest stations', of which Banbury had the first in the country. It was inspired by the sight of 1,000 thirsty troops dashing from their train one hot afternoon to drink water from the fire buckets on the platform. Thus, on 10 September 1914, the local Red Cross formed the Banbury Station Troops' Refreshment Fund, which was fully operational before the month was out. The finance for the project was raised by voluntary subscriptions and other events rather than from Red Cross funds. The project was staffed by local ladies who attended hospital trains at the station, often being called up in the middle of the night, summer and winter alike.

For example, on Friday 2 October 1914 a hospital train from Southampton conveying 130 wounded soldiers arrived at Banbury station at about 13.00. Mr Short, the stationmaster, arranged for the train to be reversed into the down bay and for half the adjacent platform to be reserved for Red Cross staff. In attendance were a dozen uniformed Red Cross nurses of the town's number 4 and 30 detachments, who boarded the train with refreshments for the wounded troops, including 'a plentiful supply of beef tea (Bovril), warm milk, tea, cakes and fruit'. Cigarettes were also distributed. The soldiers offered their thanks and reported that 'they were quite comfortable and felt very little inconvenience from the travelling of the train', which was just as well, for in half an hour it was on its way again, taking them to hospitals in Newcastle and Aberdeen.

In mid-October word spread around Banbury that a hospital train conveying severely wounded troops would call at the station. It was due at 11.45 but its departure from Southampton was delayed by an hour and a half 'owing to some of the cases on board needing serious attention before it could leave'. Thus it did not reach Banbury until 13.00, by which time a large crowd had assembled at the station to see the train; the bridge and Station Road were 'occupied by considerable numbers'. When the train arrived, it too was reversed into the bay where the Red Cross nurses were again in attendance. In some of the coaches the less seriously wounded were up and chatted with their hosts as refreshments were distributed, but the more serious cases were in bed in closed coaches which the nurses visited by 'courtesy of the officer in charge'.

The public were able to see the train and its occupants. It consisted of nine LNWR corridor parcel and mail vans 'which now bore painted on their panels a large red cross, and which had undergone a complete transformation'. Each van had been converted into a hospital ward, with sixteen beds in two tiers and one coach had been fitted out and lined with zinc to serve as a treatment ward. The men aboard were all casualties of the Battle of the Aisne, principally from

A Jumbo Class locomotive and train at Port Meadow Halt, *c.*1914. The locomotive and halt belonged to the LNWR; the GWR main line to Oxford can be seen in the background. (Courtesy of Kingfisher Postcards)

Soissons, and mostly suffering from shrapnel rather than gunshot wounds. 'One man was the proud possessor of a shrapnel bullet he had had extracted from his head', for instance. At 13.40 the hospital train left Banbury for Glasgow 'amid waving farewells' from the crowd, to which the troops 'heartily responded'.

And so it continued. On Friday 16 October, 'the GWR station at Banbury presented an appearance of great activity' – at least three hospital trains from Southampton were expected to stop here, at 10.45, 12.15 and 13.15. However, the trains were delayed and it was not until 17.00 that the first one reached Oxford, and 17.40 that it arrived at Banbury. 'It conveyed 125 convalescent wounded soldiers, mostly Belgians but a few French''. This train departed from Banbury at 18.10 but the other two did not arrive at all! On Sunday 25 October a train carrying 135 English wounded bound for Newcastle was attended by Red Cross staff while another, conveying eighty-five Belgian casualties to Lichfield (Staffs) and due at midnight, finally steamed into the station at 01.30. Another train of wounded stopped briefly at Banbury later during that Monday.

As the war went on, the number of casualties mounted. In one week alone during July 1916, following the Battle of the Somme, 47,000 sick and wounded men were landed at British ports. Considerable demands were made on Banbury's Red Cross at this time as convoys of hospital trains had to be dealt with at the railway station: on 7 July one of 350; on 11 July one of 140 and another of 212. Mr S.J. Mawle reported that the town's Red Cross Hospital, was 'filling up with wounded soldiers from France, and they will now require all the support they can get from their friends in the district'. Indeed, such support was forthcoming. For example, 'Mr Stroud has kindly allowed a portion of his field adjoining the hospital to be fenced off to provide a recreation ground and a lawn, where the patients can sit out and enjoy themselves when the weather will permit'.

During the war, Britain's railways as a whole transported over 2.5 million sick and wounded on hospital trains, which were able to carry over 8,000 casualties at any one time. Many of them travelled up the Cherwell Valley line and called at Banbury railway station. Here, in the first fortnight of its existence alone, the Troops' Refreshment Fund distributed food and drink, including 3,000 gallons of lemonade, to 35,000 men. The Fund was 'abundantly provided by several ladies and gentlemen of the town and neighbourhood'. It was a pleasure to know, Mr Mawle wrote, 'how much the wounded soldiers appreciate the comforts that our Red Cross nurses provide for them'. At Banbury station between 1914 and 1918, hundreds of thousands of sick and wounded soldiers were plied with hot beverages in winter and cool lemonade in summer.

In a sense, Britain's railways were themselves casualties of the war. 'It had been anticipated that the War would cause a considerable lessening of the ordinary passenger traffic', according to MacDermot. 'Far from it; people continued to travel for business and pleasure just as usual'. Together, the civilian and military traffic imposed a huge burden on the country's railways and 'the demands which they made for permanent way, engine power, men, and rolling stock were very considerable'. Not surprisingly, accidents happened more often. In the early months of the war there was an accident on the Cherwell Valley railway at Somerton, at 07.10 on Sunday 8 November 1914. That morning, work on the permanent way of the up line was being undertaken by men in a ballast train comprising an engine, coach and guard's van.

Suddenly, an up goods train appeared, having run past the signals against it. 'The oncoming train was travelling at a fair pace and a Somerton ganger gave a hurried warning to the occupants of the standing train and several of the workmen in the coach jumped out'. So severe was the impact as the goods train ran into the rear of the ballast train that the latter's guard's van was broken in two and the coach was wrecked. The guard, Mr Ernest Justice, sustained a bad wound on his thigh and a yard ganger, Mr John Boffin, sustained injuries to his head, shoulders and back. The injured men, from Banbury, were taken on the engine to the Oxford Infirmary. Several of the wagons on the goods train were derailed and damaged. Both tracks were closed to traffic until noon as breakdown gangs worked to repair the damaged permanent way.

Wartime traffic in general was worked under very difficult conditions, 'attributable to the acute congestion at many places' and 'the pronounced shortage of engines and men'. The Railway Executive Committee finally announced that 'the resources of the railways being already strained to the utmost, this demand could only be met if drastic reductions were made forthwith'. Consequently, on 1 January 1917 many expresses were suspended or made slower with more stops, restaurant, sleeping and slip coaches were discontinued and train mileage was reduced while fares were increased. To release staff, lots of small stations and halts were shut. The GWR had opened 145 new halts between 1904 and the outbreak of the war; between 1915 and 1917 it closed seventy-seven stations and halts, including Wolvercot Platform (opened in 1908 and closed in 1916).

In 1918, the railway trade unions put in a claim for a 10s pay rise for the men but were only granted 5s. At first the men seemed to have accepted the deal but within days a strke originated in South Wales and spread swiftly to other parts of the country. On the morning of Tuesday 24 September about a hundred of the 120 men in the locomotive department at Banbury downed tools, with the result that several local trains were either cancelled or ran late. Support was more half-hearted at Oxford, where many of the older men, especially drivers, continued to work so that several trains still ran from there. Other parts of the GWR were also affected. Two trains from London via Banbury – the 09.30 to Bimingham and the 10.30 to Birkenhead – did not run and the town's train service became increasingly disorganized as the day wore on.

Banbury was affected later in the day when the 13.17 and 13.35 trains to London, one by the Bicester cut-off and the other via Oxford, were amalgamated and set out late along the Cherwell Valley route, 'the carriages being packed'. The striking railwaymen assembled in groups during the day in the vicinity of the station and at 16.30 attended a union meeting in their clubroom at the Cricketer's Inn, Grimsbury. In the evening there were some 'lively scenes' between the strikers and wounded soldiers, who persuaded the railwaymen to allow five of their number to attend another meeting at 20.00. The soldiers listened to the views of the strikers and accepted the railwaymens' grievance about their pay but contended that the strike was inopportune and that their sacrifice was 'small compared with the sacrifices being made by the men at the front'.

On the Wednesday, through train services were fairly well maintained although some local services from Banbury were cancelled including an early train to Bicester, two stopping trains to London and the 10.40 from Oxford. At 11.00 the Chief Constable used the Defence of the Realm Act to declare picketing illegal and the precincts of the station were very quiet. Around 11.30 an 'animated altercation' took place on Banbury bridge between a postwoman and a woman munition worker, supported by several wounded soldiers, and three strikers, who 'had a lively quarter of an hour'. Locally and in many other places the strike was unpopular, and that evening a telegram was received from Cardiff where a mass meeting of railwaymen had voted to return to work. The men in the Banbury traffic department also decided to return to work immediately.

By Thursday 26 September the strike – a proverbial flash in the pan – was over and the GWR was back in business. (The GCR and LNWR had remained unaffected throughout.) 'All the men who were out have resumed work at Banbury station,' it was reported, 'and the conditions are rapidly becoming normal'. Within weeks the war itself was over too, with the armistice signed on 11 November 1918, but Britain's railways never returned to normal. More than some other companies, the GWR had borne the brunt of the war effort, increasing its goods and mineral traffic by 23% between 1913 and 1917, (compared with just 3% for the LNWR). The GWR ran 88,603 troop and munitions trains for the Government between 1914 and 1918. According to MacDermot, the Government got 'the best of the bargain made with the Railway Companies in 1914'.

Reflecting on business at the town's station in 1918, the *Banbury Guardian* commented on the demands made of the GWR's resources in dealing with the heavy military and naval traffic. Hundreds of military specials, including those of the American Expeditionary Force and the Red Cross, had to be handled in addition to the ordinary civilian trains on the Cherwell Valley railway 'between Oxford and Wolverhampton and to and from the Great Central Company's system'. All grades of staff had contributed to the efficient working of the traffic, it concluded, and the demands made on the staff 'have been met in a thoroughly patriotic manner'. Indeed, thousands of Great Western men actually joined the fighting forces – by the end of the war 25,479 of them (nearly a third of the total GWR staff) had enlisted, of whom 2,524 lost their lives.

# 15    Trouble and strife

Britaln's railways emerged from the war in a sorry state, worn out by hard work and lack of investment, but still under Government control. Increases in the cost of coal and other materials, along with higher rates and taxes, resulted in a doubling of working expenses between 1913 and 1919. Thus, in 1920, goods and mineral charges were doubled, and passenger fares raised 75% above pre-1917 levels. All in all, the rises served to drive traffic from the railways into a growing (and more competitive) road transport industry. On 19 August 1921 the country's crippled railways were released from Government control but were merged into four large groups with effect from 1 January 1923. Only the Great Western retained its pre-war identity.

Another legacy of the war years was a series of labour problems which affected the railways. The demands of the railway trade unions for higher pay and an eight-hour day were met from 1 February 1919. Further wage demands, accompanied by a strike, were settled on 5 October 1919, leaving the wages bill for 1920 at more than triple the pre-war level. By 1921 the GWR had some 110,000 employees to pay! However, the most serious labour trouble of the period – in support of the miners and affecting other industries besides the railways – was connected with the General Strike of 1926. On Sunday 2 May, the GWR was given twenty-four hours' notice by the National Union of Railwaymen that it was calling its members out on strike.

The whole country knew what to expect well in advance and the British public made the most of the following day's train services. The last train from Paddington to Oxford on the evening of 3 May was crammed with over a thousand passengers! When the strike began at midnight, employees of the LMSR (the conglomerate which had replaced the LNWR in 1923, and which also served Oxford and Banbury) gave virtually total support for the strike. On the GWR, most employees downed tools but a handful of drivers and firemen – and rather more signalmen – proved somewhat half-hearted. Whether it was because their company had retained its corporate identity or because of the actions of their General Manager is a matter of conjecture.

The GWR's General Manager, Felix Pole, had posted notices and sent telegrams to the men, asking 'Whom Do You Serve?' He declared the action to be in breach of their contracts of service and had contingency plans ready, including the recruitment of volunteers in an attempt to replace striking railwaymen and maintain some services. The GWR was London's largest supplier of milk, carried to the capital from the countryside each day in trains loaded with churns, and Pole was determined to maintain this traffic at all costs. At Oxford the striking railwaymen seemed equally determined and had organised a 'strike committee', with its headquarters at the Labour Party-funded Ruskin College. The two sides now joined in battle!

On Tuesday 5 May, the first day of the strike, the GWR and LMS railway stations at Oxford were 'in a state of almost complete desolation', reported the *Oxford Times*. At the GWR station, a few intending travellers paced the platforms and a few porters were at work amid large piles of luggage and milk churns. An official was quoted as saying, 'The men have been leaving at all times, and although there are a few working now, we don't know how long they will stay'. At Rewley Road, the LMS station, some officials were on duty but there were no signs of life on the rails. 'We have not turned a wheel this morning', one of their officials said. However, 'some signs of activity were discernable on the GWR lines' and here wheels did turn.

During the day the GWR managed to run one train to London, one to Birmingham and another to Kingham. Trains also ran on the Fairford and Wallingford branch lines. Some milk trains got through to Oxford and were 'sent on up the line'. In fact, some 8,000 churns of milk arrived in Paddington that day and were unloaded by volunteers. About 1,500 people had volunteered their labour to the GWR and the company had accepted 450 of them. By this means, the GWR announced its intention to run a skeleton service from suburban stations to Paddington the following day. In contrast, over on the LMS the strike was solid and not a single train arrived or departed after the mail train had pulled into Rewley Road at 05.40 on the Tuesday morning.

On Wednesday it was reported that 'many trains are running on the GWR'. There were trains to London at 07.10 and 11.00, while trains from Paddington to Birmingham called at Oxford at 08.10 and 10.10. Oxford was also served by the 14.30 and 15.00 trains from Paddington, *en route* to Birmingham and Worcester respectively. It was reported that all these trains were crewed 'by GWR men and not by amateurs'. On the GWR network as a whole, 194 passenger, milk and perishable trains ran on 5 May. By the next day, Thursday 6 May, several return runs were made from Paddington to Birmingham and Worcester via Oxford. The South Midland Motor Bus Company also ran a bus service between Oxford and London.

By the following week the Great Western was operating even more services in the Oxford area. For instance, on the Woodstock branch there were three Oxford-Blenheim return trains on the Monday, four on the Tuesday, and four again on the Wednesday. On that day too – 12 May – the TUC called off the General Strike unconditionally after just nine days. The GWR management rubbed salt into the strikers' wounds by refusing to re-employ them unless each man signed a form – issued by the Traffic Department at all stations – declaring: 'You are hereby re-engaged on the understanding that you are not relieved of the consequences of having broken your contract of service with the Company'. It was a sore point with the men.

Initially, the GWR strikers dug in their heels, especially at Bristol. At Oxford, following a meeting at Ruskin College on the morning of 13 May, members of the NUR and ASLEF agreed not to return to work until the Company's 'embargo' was 'done away with'. Practically all the employees remained out on that

Thursday. Of 350 Oxford men on strike, only twenty-five went in that day, mostly signalmen and none of them drivers or firemen. Far from suggesting that the General Strike was over, the 'deserted appearance' of Oxford's station that morning 'gave the impression that it was still on'. At Banbury, after a meeting on Wednesday night, the men there also objected to the form and on Thursday their strike picket was actually strengthened!

Nevertheless, the GWR managed to run 1,245 passenger, milk and perishable trains on Friday 14 May. It was clear to the strikers that they could not win. Their resistance quickly crumbled and they began to drift into work. Even then, the GWR management played cat and mouse with them, taking them back only as required, and refusing to re-employ some at all. A week later, virtually all the employees were back at work. 'London trains are normal and the local service is complete', it was claimed in Oxford, although services were not fully restored at Banbury until mid-July. The strike cost the GWR over £4 million and some economies were made to save on coal consumption, not least because the miners stayed out until Christmas, 1926.

To cope with an increasingly parlous financial situation, the GWR adopted a two-fold solution – economy and innovation. For example, as early as 1926, cost-cutting modifications were made on the Woodstock branch: locomotive-hauled trains were replaced by 'push-pull' auto-trains; much trackwork at the Blenheim terminus was lifted; the engine shed and signal box were closed; and the signalling was reduced as the branch was thereafter worked on the principle of only 'one

A branch auto-train (loco 5413) in a cutting on the Woodstock branch line between Woodstock and Shipton. (Courtesy of R.H.G. Simpson)

The Cardiff-Newcastle express passes Hook Norton station, *c*.1920. This service was inaugurated in 1906, running via the B&CDR, and became known as the 'Ports to Ports Express'. (Courtesy of Kingfisher Postcards)

Loco 3806 *County Kildare* at Kidlington with the 18.53 down local in June 1930. The track on the near side of the platform is the bay for Blenheim and Woodstock branch trains. (Courtesy of Charles Broadfoot/Mrs R. Giraud)

engine in steam' running at a time. On the other hand, the GWR extended its provision of unstaffed station platforms, or 'halts'. Locally, Shipton-on-Cherwell Halt, on the branch line, opened on 1 April 1929 while Tackley Halt, on the main line, opened on 6 April 1931.

Faced with growing economic depression, the Government passed a Development (Loans and Guarantees) Act in 1929. Grants and loans were made available for construction projects, by means of which the railway companies could improve their infrastructure and at the same time help to reduce unemployment. That year, redundant coalminers and steelworkers from South Wales arrived in Banbury to build a new gravitation hump sorting yard north of the station. Opened on 27 July, 1931, it allowed wagons to be marshalled into trains a lot more speedily than before. Some twenty sidings fanned out below the hump, each wagon rolling down into the correct one over electro-pnuematic points which were operated from a single control cabin.

The Great Western experimented with long-distance road 'feeder' bus services, running cross-country to connect with its principle express trains. One, inaugurated on 20 October 1927, ran between Oxford and Cheltenham; another, inaugurated on 1 July 1929, between Banbury and Swindon. These bus services were not well supported, however, and were taken over by the Black and White Bus Company in 1932. From 1933, the GWR began building diesel 'railcars' which were more economical to operate than steam locomotives. Several were based at Oxford and worked on both main and branch lines, including a novel

Bloxham station, *c.*1930, looking towards Banbury. The railwayman standing by the trolley loaded with milk churns is possibly Mr Lloyd, the stationmaster. (Courtesy of Lens of Sutton)

through service between Banbury and Swindon which brought railcars into the Cherwell Valley.

Britain's longest-distance train service in this period also passed along the Cherwell Valley. A daily service of 785 miles between Aberdeen and Penzance, it comprised through carriages – including sleepers – attached to other trains. This service had been inaugurated in 1921 and launched with much publicity. Journalists were entertained for four days on end while they made the trip from Aberdeen and back, including twenty-four hours' 'recovery time' at Penzance! Another long-distance service passed through Banbury but traversed the B&CDR across the Cotswolds on its way between Swansea and Newcastle. Originating from 1906, it had been named the 'Ports to Ports Express' and in the 1930s was the prestige train of the line.

The efforts made to ensure the smooth running of this crack express were remembered by an old railwayman in later years. During the arctic winter of 1937-1938, Ray Knibbs was a locomotive fireman based at Gloucester's GWR engine shed: 'One night during a raging blizzard I was called out at 1 a.m. to report for snow plough duty. My driver, a hard man named Alf Hopkins, and I boarded engine No. 2247, a small tender type with an open cab, to which was attached a great snow plough. Picking up some thirty permanent-way men in a break-down van *en route*, we arrived at Notgrove station, high in the Cotswolds'. Facing them was a downhill cutting, forty feet deep and five miles in length, which was completely blocked by a snow drift.

Notgrove was indeed a bleak place at the best of times, being the highest through station on the GWR. 'All night we heaved and reversed, the men either side of us digging like the devil', recalls fireman Knibbs. 'Our gaffer, Fred Smith, giving instructions from the footplate, fell off. When the lamps were brought, all that could be seen was Fred's black bowler on the snow!' As the night wore on, the line was gradually cleared through to Bourton-on-the-Water, where gaffer Smith put a bottle of Scotch into the tea urn. Eventually, along came the 'Ports to Ports Express', with 'the men all cheering and whistles a-blowing, dead on schedule'. That was how the GWR beat the blizzards. To nineteen-year-old fireman Knibbs it was all 'a great adventure'.

For all its hardships, railway employment did offer reasonable security and remuneration. In the Banbury region, for example, where farm labourers typically earned less than £1.50 a week in the mid-1930s, railwaymen were better off than many other workers. A job on the railways was much sought after and the companies often took their new recruits from among the families of existing employees. So it was for one youngster who joined the Great Western at Banbury in this period. He was the son of a GWR goods guard who had moved to the town from Cheltenham – at the other end of the B&CDR – and lived in Middleton Road, Grimsbury. Born in 1923, Ken Ashton entered service with the GWR on 30 September 1937.

As a fourteen-year-old, Ken Ashton began his railway career as a 'booking lad' in the telegraph office on the down platform at Banbury station, being paid the

Loco 6354 on passenger 'pilot' duty at Banbury station, *c*.1934. The fireman (right) is Tom Morbey, the driver unknown. (Courtesy of Ron Morbey)

Tom Morbey, driving on his first turn after being 'made up' to engine driver at Banbury, *c*.1936. (Courtesy of Ron Morbey)

princely sum of 14s (70p) a week. The station at this time was 'a filthy old place', he recalls. It was still the original broad-gauge edifice, with its overall roof, but by now it was in a sorry state of repair, being 'reinforced with wooden beams'. The following year brought a transfer to Banbury Junction Signal Box as a 'booking lad' to signalman Cyril Timms. Eight months later, his next move was to the Yard Master's Office as a 'call boy' but on his sixteenth birthday he was transferred back to the signal box. In spite of all the transfers, 'in those days you still thought you had a job for life'.

For railwaymen everywhere – and the population as a whole – international events were about to bring drastic changes to their lives. It was now 1939 and the threat of war was very real, following the Munich Crisis of the previous year. Much planning and preparatory work had already been undertaken since the setting up of the Railway Technical Committee in 1937, and arrangements had already been made to place Britain's railways in the control of a Railway Executive Committee (created in 1938) should the need arise. By May 1939 the GWR had begun taking Air Raid Precautions and was already distributing 6,000 Anderson shelters a week. It was Hitler's invasion of Poland in the early hours of Friday 1 September 1939 that signalled war.

Immediately, a long-standing plan to evacuate civilians from London and other cities was put into effect. The GWR had fifty twelve-coach sets marshalled ready to convey Londoners to country districts. These were worked from Ealing Broadway between 08.30 and 17.30 daily from 1 September. On that day alone, fifty-eight trains left the capital, carrying 44,000 evacuees to safety. Oxfordshire was one of their destinations and thousands found temporary homes in Cherwell Valley towns and villages. In total, the city of Oxford expected 16,000 and the Banbury and Abingdon districts 5,000 each, with smaller towns and villages taking 2,000-3,000. Carefully laid plans of recent months were activated, the city and county authorities 'working at top speed'.

Yet again, Ruskin College was pressed into use, this time as the City of Oxford Maternity Hospital for Evacuees. The Chief Evacuation Officer, Mr Stuart Swift, had a fleet of 150 buses ready at Oxford railway station when the train conveying the 'advance guard' of evacuees steamed in just after 10.00 on Friday morning, the city being one of the first places in Britain to be at the receiving end of the mass exodus. The 800 children on the train were from East Acton, Old Oak and Shepherd's Bush. By the end of the day, Oxford stationmaster Mr Frank Buckingham had received 4,000 children and their teachers along with 'several hospital trains mostly composed of patients on stretchers in cattle trucks, smelling most unhealthy in the heat'.

On the afternoon of 1 September, trainloads of evacuees arrived elsewhere in the county: 800 in Banbury, 800 at Chipping Norton, 270 at Kidlington (arriving via Bicester station) and so on. Those arriving at Banbury station were issued with emergency rations at nearby Andy's Garage! Over the next few days, further trainloads of evacuees arrived in the Cherwell Valley. Banbury received 800 on Saturday, 1,600 on Sunday and 800 more on Monday, for example. By Sunday, so

CHIPPING NORTON GWR.
1/9/39.

Chipping Norton railway station on 1 September 1939, with the first train-load of evacuees arriving.

many had flooded into Oxford that some had to be sent back to the capital and Oxford's mayor, Dr H.T. Gillett, appealed for further accommodation to billet evacuees. By Tuesday 5 September it was reported that over 13,000 had arrived in the city.

On Sunday 3 September 1939 the people of Oxfordshire (along with the rest of the country) listened to the broadcast declaring that Britain was officially 'at war with Germany'. There was an immediate increase in rail traffic: on 4 September the GWR ran 320 troop trains plus 350 stores and ammunition trains, while others 'evacuated' meat and butter from London to cold stores in the rural areas. Ironically, as Britain mobilized and men of the British Expeditionary Force made their way south to the ports of embarkation, passenger train services were reduced. Air raid precautions were put into effect, with blackout regulations on the railways meaning that station lighting was reduced to dim blue bulbs. Platform edges were therefore whitened to assist passengers in the dark.

In this war, the RAF played a larger role, flying from bases throughout Britain. There were several in the Cherwell Valley, including a large airfield near Kidlington which had been a civilian flying school in the 1930s. Like most local airfields, it was a training establishment equipped with Hawker Harts, Harvards and Airspeed Oxfords. Even training had its dangers, as an incident in the early months of the war showed. On 14 March 1940 Harvard trainer number P5784 from Kidlington airfield crashed into a bridge on the Woodstock branch at 1 mile 50 chains (near

Shipton-on-Cherwell village). The pilot, D.S. Dadson, was killed. His body was trapped in the wrecked aircraft overnight and a guard placed on it until daylight when it could be removed.

On the whole, however, the initial months of the war were strangely quiet, for this was the period known as the 'phoney war' – many of the evacuated Londoners even began to drift back to their homes in the capital. But it was not to last. From the spring of 1940, the German advance across Europe relentlessly pushed the Allies back to the Channel, trapping the BEF and French armies at Dunkirk. At very short notice, Britain's railways took part in the evacuation, helping to bring 330,000 troops to safety between 29 May and 4 June. The GWR contributed six of its ferries to the 'small ships fleet' and forty sets of coaches to a 'pool' of trains used to take the troops to inland bases, fanning out by different routes from the ports on the south coast.

During the seven days of the Dunkirk operation, the Great Western ran 293 special trains conveying a total of over 180,000 men. Trainloads of the troops evacuated from Dunkirk were transported north along the Cherwell Valley line. Many of them threw messages out as they passed through local stations, hoping that telegraph staff would relay them to their families to let them know they were safe. To accommodate the men, reception areas were hurriedly created, including a temporary tented base on Port Meadow, north of Oxford. Those evacuees who had gone back to London now returned to the comparative safety of rural Oxfordshire too, as it became evident that the 'phoney war' was over and the real war was about to start.

# 16   War and peace

The Second World War, like the first, made huge demands of the nation's railways, imposing even greater burdens than its predecessor. Despite the reduction in services and attempts to limit civilian use, passenger travel increased during the war and overcrowding became a notorious problem on those trains that still ran. The coaches on some trains were reported to be so weighed down that 'their springs were flattened to a degree which resulted in running boards fouling station platforms while the trains were in motion', as civilian passengers found themselves shoulder to shoulder with soldiers and sailors in packed trains.

Nationally, the railways of Britain carried 70% more passengers and 50% more freight in wartime than in peacetime. Locally, the Great Western main line between Oxford and Banbury became a vital railway artery between the supply factories of the industrial north and the 'front line' near the south coast. The Cherwell Valley railway had a strategic importance in the war efforts made on the 'Home Front', being subject to the effect of warfare for the next five years as it was worked to its limits. Between 1939 and 1945 more freight traffic passed along the Cherwell Valley line than the route could bear but somehow it coped.

Oxford station became even more of a bottleneck for trains than usual and, as passenger trains had priority, southbound goods trains were often held in the long loop line stretching from Wolvercot Junction almost to Oxford station. During the busy war years a queue of heavy freight 2-8-0 locomotives pulling goods trains of up to 100 wagons regularly queued engine-to-guard's van in the loop. They simmered there for hours on end, until they could be released one at a time to trundle through the 'centre road' at the station and on to their destinations. In this respect, the demands of the Second World War were not unlike the First.

A critical difference this time, however, was the added problem of aerial warfare and bombing. During August and September 1940 the Battle of Britain took place in the skies over South-east England, being followed by the London Blitz. German aircraft regularly flew over Oxfordshire but rarely dropped bombs, although on 1 November 1940 a lone raider did drop four bombs on Kidlington airfield, destroying two Harvard trainers and damaging a hangar. Of course, anti-aircraft guns were used against Luftwaffe raiders and on one occasion a stray Messerschmitt 109 was shot down over Oxford station, crashing near the engine shed.

The engine shed at Oxford presented a prime target to the Luftwaffe, since it was a Victorian relic dating from 1862 and constructed from tarred timber. Following Dunkirk, workers were encouraged to form Local Defence Volunteer units (renamed the Home Guard from July, 1940) and so driver Albert King, a First World War veteran, established a unit at Oxford engine shed under his command. Not surprisingly in the circumstances, their duties included fire-watching and air raid precautions. For use in air raids, the unit had four 20mm anti-aircraft cannon at their disposal around the loco yard, but these were never fired in anger.

Apart from this the Oxford engine shed Home Guard unit had a large potential membership but few weapons. The 130 volunteer enginemen there had just one Lee-Enfield rifle, to be shared by one and all when on duty! The story is told (by Adrian Vaughan, in *Grime and Glory*) that they acquired a second rifle, thus doubling their armoury, after signalmen between Banbury and Oxford spotted another Lee-Enfield rifle lying in a truck full of rubbish on a goods train travelling south along the Cherwell Valley line. Word was passed along the line from box to box so that Albert King was able to claim the weapon when the goods train stopped in the loop near Oxford engine shed.

In anticipation of air raids putting cross-London railway lines out of action, a new 'ring-route' was created in a fifty-mile radius of the capital. It was based on the LMSR Oxford-Cambridge line, to which new connections were made, including a brand new double-track link constructed between the GWR and LMSR half a mile north of Oxford station. A new signal box was built here at the same time and came into operation as 'Oxford North Junction Box' on 30 November 1940. To increase traffic-handling facilities further, the northbound loop line was extended from Oxford North to Wolvercot Junction, opening on 3 March 1942.

Oxford station's north signal box, with its 100-lever frame. Here,in 1949, signalmen Jerry Trevis (by the frame) and Boris Marchant (under the clock) are on duty. The booking boy is Peter Hemmings. (Courtesy of R.H.G. Simpson)

A general view of Banbury loco shed, *c.*1960.

The existing goods yard north of Oxford engine shed soon proved inadequate for wartime requirements and so an extensive new goods yard was constructed south of the station, at Hinksey. Here, 1,000 wagons could be accommodated in sidings either side of the main line. To control the sidings two more new signal boxes were built – Hinksey South Box, opened on 29 March, 1942, was built by Italian prisoners of war. The old goods yard was later closed and the land vacated was used to enlarge Oxford engine shed and carriage sidings, including a new coaling stage. This work was not completed until New Year, 1945.

Wartime conditions were making similar demands at the Banbury end of the Cherwell Valley line. Banbury's engine shed was relatively modern, having replaced a shed of 1889 vintage. It dated from the period before the First World War when, with the Woodford link and Bicester cut-off, Banbury had expanded as a railway centre in its own right. Situated south of the station, the loco shed was an Edwardian construction opened in late summer, 1908. As built, it was a four track brick shed, complete with a coaling stage and a 55ft turntable. The shed received a wartime extension, including lifting shops and ash-clearing sheds, in 1944.

In the 1930s Banbury loco shed had provided steady employment to over 120 enginemen but upon the outbreak of the Second World War circumstances changed. The total number of staff employed by the GWR rose by 13% (from 99,223 to 112,102) between 1939 and 1945. However, this was far less than the increase in traffic and there was still an urgent need for extra manpower – or womanpower! Like other industries, the Great Western took to recruiting large numbers of women and by 1943 there were some 16,000 women employed on the GWR in various grades. In such conditions, there were opportunities for rapid promotion.

Young Ken Ashton, who had joined the GWR at Banbury less than two years earlier, applied for a transfer to the engine shed in the summer of 1940. He was summoned to Great Western headquarters at Park House, Swindon, on 1 June for the compulsory medical examination and made the return journey by train with a group of other hopefuls. 'About eight of us went down, all young chaps around sixteen years of age. The doctor examined us and later we all heard that we'd passed'. All of the young men concerned were made up to engine cleaners and began work together at Banbury loco not many weeks afterwards.

Ken Ashton recalls his first day as an engine cleaner at Banbury shed on Monday 15 July 1940:'I started with great apprehension because it was a filthy, dirty job'. Cleaners worked in a gang under a leading cleaner and progressed to cleaning different parts of locomotives with seniority. To polish the copper and brass rims around chimneys and safety valves, 'you climbed onto the engine and stood on the handrail of the boiler – it was a bit dicey really!' At this date, Banbury was home to around fifty locomotives, ranging from small 0-6-0 tank engines to large 4-6-0 tender engines, and each gang cleaned about six engines a day.

Not long after Ken Ashton started work, the Luftwaffe began its air raids on the Midlands. It was on Tuesday 13 August that the city of Birmingham got its first taste of aerial warfare. The German bombers passed over Banbury but seldom bothered the men working at the loco shed – firedroppers carried on cleaning red-hot ash from engines out in the open. Inside the shed there was a blackout in force at night, making the work even more difficult and dangerous. A frightening task Ken Ashton remembers is working under an engine in the darkened shed, in among the moving parts, with only a dirty 'Not to be Moved' sign fixed to it for protection!

On 3 October the Luftwaffe bombed Banbury gasworks while Ken Ashton was on duty at the shed. 'I had to take a message to driver Alfie Grant at Grimsbury. While I was there, I saw a German plane come out of the clouds. At first I thought he was dropping leaflets but it was bombs: they hit the gasworks, close to the shed, the goods shed and the track in front of the signal box, narrowly missing the box itself but causing casualties. When I got back to the yard I saw a huge bomb on a pile of gravel and the south end shunters, standing at the door of the air raid shelter, shouted at me to get away quickly because it might still go off'.

He had another close shave while on night duty at the engine shed, when Banbury was bombed again. 'We heard the whistle of a bomb coming down close by: we all crouched down, waiting for it to explode, expecting it to hit the shed. Then we heard a thud nearby as the bomb blew out the lock gate on the canal nearby – a million to one chance!'. He knows that Banbury got off lightly, however, compared with the Midlands cities. On Thursday 14 November he was again working on the night shift when 'a stream of German bombers' flew across and later saw 'a glow in the sky over Coventry' as they dropped their bombs there.

Loco 3216 at Banbury Hump Yard in around 1950. On the left is shunter Wallace Ashton, father of Ken. The Hump Yard opened in 1931 and closed in 1970. (Courtesy of Ken Ashton)

In the spring of 1941, Ken Ashton was promoted to goods fireman at Banbury loco, going straight onto the shunting link and working the hump yard pilot. 'I shall always remember my first shift. My driver was new too, having just been made up from fireman, and we spent the night at the yard with a 37XX tank engine, pushing wagons over the hump'. Trains ran in from Woodford and Birmingham and as they got up to the hump the main line engines uncoupled and went off to the shed for servicing. 'Then we'd buffer our little tankie up to the back of the train and shunt the wagons, to form new trains for mainline locos to take onward'.

After about twelve months of shunting work, fireman Ashton was promoted to main line goods trains. During the war, much of the time was spent in loops waiting for faster trains to pass, but this had its compensations. Mealtimes on the footplate were eagerly awaited, often consisting of an egg and bacon 'fry-up' cooked on the fireman's shovel in the firebox. Sometimes alternatives presented themselves. Looking into a field while waiting in a loop one night, fireman Ashton and his driver, George Styles, spotted a stoat with a rabbit, which was swiftly 'liberated' by the driver and brought back to be cooked and eaten on the footplate.

As the war dragged on and food became scarcer, opportunities to add to the domestic mealtable were often found while at work on the railway. On one occasion, while held in Astrop loop south of Banbury, fireman Ashton was able

Spend your holidays at home – free the Railways
for Forces and urgent war materials.

# BRITISH RAILWAYS

GWR ——— LMS ——— LNER ——— SR

## No Additional Trains at Christmas

The Minister of War Transport has directed that no more passenger trains are to be run on any ordinary day between 21st and 29th December (inclusive) than on any ordinary day in December.

The public is warned that, if more people seek to travel than can be accommodated, they will find themselves stranded.

> **NO RESTAURANT CARS OR BUFFET CARS**
> will be run in England and Wales between
> December 21st and 29th, inclusive.

**BRITISH**  **RAILWAYS**

RAILWAY EXECUTIVE COMMITTEE

In order to free up the rail system for military use the government issued public information ads like these two and those on the opposite page.

*"Is your journey really necessary?"*

LIGHTER
LUGGAGE
PLEASE!

## IF YOU **MUST** TRAVEL

Your journey will be more
comfortable if you take
only a little luggage

You will help to reduce
congestion and avoid delay

Take sufficient refreshments
to cover your train journey

**HELP THE RAILWAYS TO HELP YOU**

**BRITISH RAILWAYS**
GWR — LMS — LNER — SR

WHITSUN
TRAINS
*are going to the front!*

We are on the eve of great events.
Now—more than ever—every available train is needed for the massing
of war materials for the battlefronts.
Victory—and the lives of our men—
depend on these supplies.

## DON'T TRAVEL AT WHITSUN

**RAILWAY EXECUTIVE COMMITTEE**

to fill a sack with tomatoes from a field beside the line. On another occasion he was firing a mixed goods train to Leamington which was put into the loop at Fosse Road so that the midnight mail from Paddington could overtake. 'It was a bright moonlit night and as I looked across the field I could see all these white shapes – I ran down the bank and managed to pick a good few pounds of mushrooms'.

On 4 March 1943 Ken Ashton had a pay rise and now earned 63s (£3.15) a week. There were times when the money was hard earned. In the war all locomotives were fitted with blackout sheets to cover the cab at night. However, this was the time when most goods trains were run because there were few passenger trains for them to impede. In these conditions, it became even more difficult to work long and heavy freight trains. The heaviest freights operated from Banbury were the trains of ironstone destined for steelworks in Wales and the Midlands, which were made up of twenty-ton hoppers and could total 1,000 tons per train.

Ken Ashton recalls working an ironstone train to Margam via Leamington as far as Stratford, where Banbury crews were relieved. 'We had a 28XX class heavy freight loco with a full load and were almost there', but on the 'exceptionally steep' (1 in 75) gradient down from Wilmcote the signals were against them. Driver Dick Gardiner applied the vacuum brake on the engine and fireman Ashton wound down the tender brake but the guard didn't seem to have his brake on. 'The train ran away, shooting past danger signals and into Stratford station. If there had been a passenger train at the platform it would have been a catastrophe!'

The heavy burden imposed on Britain's railway system reached its peak in 1944, when the Allies prepared for and carried out the D-Day invasion. During that year, the nation's railways ran 178,000 special military trains for the Government, almost a third of the total number run in the whole six years of the war. In the two-month build-up that started in March, there were 24,000 special trains in all, carrying 230,000 troops. In the three-weeks immediately prior to D-Day, some 9,679 specials were run by Britain's railway companies as the Allied forces gathered on the south coast, ready to return to the continent and win the war.

As before, the Great Western played a major role in the military operation. The huge build-up of supplies for the D-Day landings in Europe resulted in tremendous traffic on the Cherwell Valley line. Goods movements through Oxford, for example, reached an all-time record in April 1944, when in just one week over 1,200 freight and military trains passed through the area. Smaller stations were also affected. Kidlington was heavily used in the build-up and the GWR was called upon to send six-ton mobile cranes to the station (probably to handle traffic for the nearby RAF airfield) in June 1944, the critical D-Day month.

The railway system was responsible for the continuous movement of military supplies to south coast ports throughout the invasion operation. Moreover, the

Allied troops arriving in Britain at west coast ports such as Liverpool and Glasgow had to be conveyed to the south coast by rail as swiftly as possible. The GWR played its part in moving thousands of American GIs from ports on the Mersey and the Clyde to the other end of the country. Railwaymen everywhere worked on relief shifts, doing longer hours than ever and undertaking duties of all sorts to ensure that the military specials and troop trains got through to their destinations.

At Banbury, fireman Ashton, still officially a goods fireman, was often required to work as passenger fireman on the footplate of 4-6-0 locomotives hauling troop trains. He recalls working one from Banbury to Frome via Oxford, with a 49XX Hall loco. As with any train conveying GIs, after reaching the destination the engine crew made a point of searching for leftover kit – 'we found lots of coffee' – before taking the empty stock back to Banbury. Sometimes, when loco coal was short and of poor quality, their empty stock trains only just made it back to Banbury, 'with the tender almost empty and two foot of clinker under the firebox door!'

During the final year of the war Britain's railways not only carried thousands of troops but thousands more civilian travellers too: nationally, passenger travel was greater in volume in the last six months of wartime than it had been in peacetime. This was evident in the case of the Cherwell Valley main line. For example, at Kidlington station, 7,550 tickets had been issued in 1934, and the number rose to 22,373 in 1944, (the total was 19,494 in 1945). However, it was a different story on the branch lines – at Blenheim & Woodstock station 22,169 tickets had been issued in 1934, but here the number fell to 19,782 in 1944 and to 17,527 in 1945.

One day in the spring of 1945, the people of Oxfordshire (along with the rest of the country) listened to broadcast messages indicating that the war was over. The official peace declaration came the next day, 8 May – VE Day – which was observed as a public holiday in towns and villages across the county. Everywhere, flags and bunting were put up to decorate houses, shops and streets. In Banbury on that Tuesday evening, a bonfire of tar barrels was lit in the recreation ground by the river, watched by crowds on Banbury bridge, and as darkness fell Banbury Cross was floodlit for the first time since the blackout began. Peace had returned.

When VE day arrived, the nation's railways were worn out, having been stretched to their limits in wartime. A massive investment programme was clearly necessary and the form it would take was determined by the outcome of the general election held as soon as the war finished: the Labour Government which was elected proposed nationalisation of Britain's railways. Precise details were later enshrined in a Transport Act in 1947, including compulsory purchase of the railways by the state and the creation of a new management body, the British Transport Commission, to take control of the system with effect from 1 January 1948.

For a while things went on much as before. The GWR carried on building steam engines, including a new batch of 'Castle' class 4-6-0 locomotives.

Number 5099 *Compton Castle* hauled the royal train on 24 October 1946 when King George VI and Queen Elizabeth came to Oxford to open the new Bodleian Library. Decorations put up at the station to greet them were transferred during the day from the platform at which they arrived to the one from which they departed that evening. It is interesting to note that the city councillors who greeted the royal couple included six Great Western railwaymen, one of them the mayor.

Under the 1947 Act, the country's railways were to be a single entity, British Railways, based on six regions, with the GWR becoming the Western Region. Until the Act took effect, the railway companies struggled on as things went from bad to worse. The coal supply situation remained difficult in the face of an ongoing post-war national fuel crisis, which was made worse by the appalling winter of 1946-7. A great freeze-up started on 28 January, being followed weeks later by a thaw which caused severe flooding. Although not for the first time, the Great Western line was completely submerged by floodwater at Hinksey, south of Oxford.

At last, at midnight on Tuesday 31 December 1947, the private railway companies officially ceased to exist. Just five minutes after Big Ben had struck midnight to mark the start of 1948, locomotive number 5032, *Usk Castle*, left for Birkenhead with the first British Railways train to depart from Paddington, Western Region. In reality, there were few noticeable differences as a result of nationalisation until long after 1948. On coaches, GWR chocolate-and-cream livery gave way to BR red-and-cream but GWR officers, practices and equipment carried on 'business as usual'. The Great Western Railway didn't die – instead it faded away.

# 17  A national concern

As a national concern, British Railways also became an entity about which the nation *was* concerned. Having acquired a worn-out infrastructure from the old private companies, the new public management body, the Transport Commission, was given the task of turning the country's railway network into an efficient system of public transport. However, in the austere post-war years this was to prove a long and difficult process: money for new investment was scarce, prices were rising and there were shortages of materials. Further fuel crises in 1950 and 1951 only made the problems worse but the commission had been instructed from the outset that rail services had to pay for themselves; even meeting the wages bill was a strain on resources.

At Banbury, soon after the war ended, the GWR had promoted fireman Ken Ashton to the passenger link and given him annual pay rises (30 July 1945 – 74s 6d, 1 July 1946 – 102s 6d, 30 June 1947 – 110s). Under British Railways his pay was increased to 117s (£5.85) a week from 1 February 1948. In this period, his regular duties included firing 14XX or 54XX class engines with autocar trains on the High Wycombe and Kingham services. He was normally paired with driver Bert Gardner and their usual locomotives were 1458, 1473, 5405 and 5407. Sometimes they worked a Cherwell Valley line passenger train to Oxford or Didcot, another back to Leamington with a 63XX class engine, and came home to Banbury as passengers themselves.

One of the passenger turns operated from Banbury was a daily workmen's train to serve the motor works at Morris Cowley, on the line from Oxford to Princes Risborough. Ironically, the car factories soon began to attract men away from railway employment. Fireman Ashton himself recalls: 'My brother-in-law was employed at Cowley works and when I saw his pay packet it was twice what I was getting on the railway'. By now he was married (his wife was one of the evacuees from London who had come to the Banbury area in 1939) and had started a family. Faced with new responsibilities but having had no pay rise for over two years he was tempted to join the growing number of railwaymen then working in the factories at Cowley.

'We hadn't had the pay increases other people had. That's what influenced me to leave, but it was a shame really because, after I left, the railway improved its rates and came into line with the factory'. Nevertheless, Ken Ashton resigned from British Railways, working his last shift at Banbury shed on Saturday 9 September 1950. He was one of many. Between 1950 and 1957, for instance, the peak years, there were three links at Banbury shed without firemen. The loco crews who left the Western Region – at Banbury, Oxford and elsewhere – went to work in places such as the Cowley car factories, with higher wages and more suitable hours of work. As a result of staff shortages, it became increasingly difficult to maintain train services.

Ken Ashton is the fireman here (left) with loco 5404 at Banbury station. This photograph was taken around 1950, shortly before Ken resigned from British Railways. (Courtesy of Ken Ashton)

For reasons of economy, the British Transport Commission started to withdraw unremunerative rail services. Between 1948 and 1959 it closed 2,944 miles of the country's railways, either to passenger services only or to all traffic. An early casualty in the Cherwell Valley area was the section of B&CD line from Kings Sutton to Chipping Norton, from which passenger services were withdrawn in 1951. The stations to be closed were Adderbury, Milton Halt, Bloxham, Hook Norton and Rollright Halt. Chipping Norton reverted to being the terminus of a branch line from Kingham but retained its passenger service. Freight services continued on the section concerned until all services were withdrawn from the B&CD line on 15 October, 1962.

For the stations affected in 1951, the final day of passenger services was Saturday 2 June. The last stopping train was the 17.20 from Kingham, a locomotive propelling a single carriage, on the front of which was placed a Union Jack, a laurel wreath and a placard inscribed: 'Last Train, 1887-1951'. The engine was crewed by driver Bernard Townsend and fireman Doug Baker, both of Banbury shed, with Mr B. Sims as guard. Also on the train were Mr G.W. Holland, Banbury shedmaster, and Mr W. Parnell, Divisional Locomotive Inspector. A party of boys from Bloxham School, which had been served by the line, had made the outward journey on an earlier train and were now travelling back in the care of a house-master, Mr D.G. Longdon.

At Bloxham, crowds assembled at the station half an hour before the train was due and the platforms were soon packed. Cheers were raised when the first puff of smoke from the approaching train was sighted and in an adjacent field cricketers stopped to witness an historic moment. Among those on the platform was seventy-seven-year-old George Manning, who had travelled on the *first* train from Bloxham. Now he boarded the *last* train, having been promised that he could keep his ticket as a souvenir when he got to Banbury. As the departing train gathered speed, it exploded several detonators which had been put on the rails but the last sound those on the train heard from Bloxham station was the sound of a bugle playing 'One More Mile to Go'.

Also in June 1951 came a bombshell concerning the Woodstock branch line, when the *Oxford Mail* reported that it was a candidate for closure. The report predicted 'considerable opposition' from farmers and others in the district, which did in fact materialize and delay the inevitable, but the traffic statistics were grim. A service of eight trains each way still ran over the branch each weekday but on average each train carried only five or six passengers – some trains actually ran empty! There were numerous objectors to the closure proposal and an intriguing idea from the Railway Development Association to operate the branch more economically by using 'railbuses', but it was to no avail. The line was destined to be closed to all traffic early in 1954.

The last day of services on the Woodstock branch – Saturday 27 February – was cold but sunny, bringing out large crowds including members of the Oxford

Loco 1420 at Woodstock on the last day of train service. The inscription chalked on the engin's tank reads: *'Fair Rosamund*, killed by Govt. R.I.P.'. (Courtesy of R.H.G. Simpson.

The last day of service, 27 February 1954, with loco 1420 calling at Shipton-on-Cherwell Halt. Later in the day, an extra coach was added to cope with passenger demand. (Courtesy of R.H.G. Simpson)

University Railway Society. Services were operated by engine number 1420 and an auto-trailer, with an extra coach being added at midday to cater for passenger demand. The final service of the day was timed to depart at 19.10 and was crewed by driver Harry Collins and fireman Jack Loveridge, both of Oxford shed, with Mr C. Watkins as guard. Also on the footplate was retired driver Bill Pomeroy, who had worked on the branch from 1906 to 1939. Among the passengers was eighty-six-year-old Mr C.W. Costar, who had worked on building the line and travelled on the first train.

Hordes of enthusiasts gathered on the platforms at Woodstock to witness the departure of the last train and 150 tickets were sold to those intending to travel on it. A Union Jack and a wreath were placed on the front of the leading carriage and various inscriptions were chalked on number 1420, including 'Cheerio', 'Born May 19th 1890, died February 27th 1954', 'Killed by Govt R.I.P.' and the misnomer 'Fair Rosamund'. As the train steamed away, it set off a barrage of detonators which had been placed on the tracks, and more exploded as it reached Shipton-on-Cherwell Halt. All the way to Kidlington (and Oxford) cameras clicked and flashbulbs lit up the evening darkness, recording the death throes of the Blenheim & Woodstock branch line.

To cut costs, British Railways also began to close stations which duplicated existing facilities. In Oxford, the ex-LNWR Rewley Road terminus was closed on 1 October, 1951, and its services redirected into the GWR's Botley Road station. The building was 'listed' and in 1999 was removed to the Buckinghamshire

Railway Centre at Quainton. Oxford's LNWR loco shed had closed on 3 December 1950 and was finally demolished in 1962. In Banbury, the ex-LNWR Merton Street terminus received a stay of execution and an experimental diesel railcar service was introduced in an attempt to generate custom. However, the station – and the line to Bletchley which it served – was eventually closed to passenger services on 31 December 1960.

It was not all doom and gloom, however. In 1955, *Modernisation and Re-equipment of British Railways* was published, and on the Western Region the first scheme of improvement undertaken as part of it was the rebuilding of Banbury station. In 1938 the GWR had decided to rebuild its original timber station but when the war broke out work was deferred. The overall roof was removed in 1952 – before it fell down! – and by now Banbury station was seen by passengers and railwaymen alike as a 'plague-spot'. An ancient wooden edifice with just two through tracks, it was 'infinitely dirty' and a major bottleneck on a busy route. Rebuilding work was effected between 1956 and 1958, making the station 'the peer of anything else in the town'.

Banbury's new railway station was a reinforced concrete frame structure, with a main building at ground level which included a booking office, left-luggage counter and bookstall. It was linked to the platforms by a 40ft-wide covered bridge housing refreshment and waiting rooms. 'The style of the buildings is modern, with the accent on cleanliness, light and fresh air', reported the *Railway Magazine*. At the same time, improvements in the track layout resulted in the

Loco crew improvement classes at Banbury, c.1957. Ron Morbey is on the left, Stan Claridge on the right, and Eric Brain (class instructor) in the centre. (Courtesy of Ron Morbey)

realignment of the main lines (and the lifting of a permanent speed restriction), the creation of four through tracks along with adequate bay accommodation, and the entire reconstruction of the station forecourt. Banbury's new station was centrally heated and lighted by fluorescent lamps.

At the other end of the Cherwell Valley, the ex-GWR station – named 'Oxford General' by British Railways – was less fortunate. Dating from 1852, some alterations had been made when the broad gauge was removed twenty years later and major remodelling was effected in 1890-1891, when the original overall roof was removed. In 1908 the platforms were extended and the track layout modified, but in other respects Oxford was still a Victorian station. Moreover, it was totally unsuited to cope with the traffic it had to handle. In 1954, the *Railway Magazine* declared: 'The problem of unavoidable delay to trains has reached such proportions as to excite comment in the national Press, and give the station a notoriety far outside Oxford itself'.

By the late 1950s Oxford station was used by 176 trains daily, fifty-four starting, fifty-two terminating and fifty calling. Its four tracks and two main platforms were barely adequate, especially when engines, carriages or parcels vans had to be changed. The centre tracks were useful for through trains but did not prevent congestion – at one time in August 1957 the line from Oxford to Banbury stations was full, with a train occupying every section. Delays to northbound trains often resulted in unscheduled stops alongside the cemetery south of the station, resulting in letters to *The Times* in which university types wittily suggested it was a form of 'ritual ancestor worship'. The station still handled 4,000 trunks and 800 bicycles for them twice-termly in 1958!

LMR engine 45116 passing the cemetery south of Oxford station with a down express in 1964 – but not stopping for ancestor worship! (Courtesy of David Canning)

At the start of the 1960s, however, it was not too much traffic but too little that was a cause of concern to the Government, which appointed Dr Richard Beeching to look into the problem. In 1963 he reported in *The Reshaping of British Railways* that the network had made its first loss – of £16.5 million – in 1956, trebling it to £48.1 million by 1958. He noted that in 1961 British Railways had some 7,000 stations, half of which produced only 2% of the total traffic. By contrast, a quarter of the total traffic receipts originated from just thirty-four stations. It was evident that something must be done, and quickly. His solution, featured under the headline 'Beeching's Axe Drops' in the *Oxford Mail,* meant the chop for nearly 2,000 stations and 5,000 route miles.

The 'Beeching Report' contained 148 pages of recommendations, including the withdrawal of 266 passenger services nationwide. It recommended the closure of 1,928 stations, in addition to 435 which British Railways had already closed or intended to close. North of Banbury, for example, Chacombe Road and Eydon Road halts on the Woodford line, and Cropredy station on the Birmingham line, had all been closed in 1956. Every station between Oxford and Leamington – except for Banbury – was recommended for closure, along with the Banbury-Woodford service and the whole ex-GCR line north of Aylesbury. Nationally, Dr Beeching hoped to secure 70% of the closures by the end of 1964, thus eliminating the railway's deficit by 1970.

Also recommended was the continuing replacement of steam by diesel engines. This change had begun with the 'Modernisation Plan'. The diesel locomotive fleet had grown from 452 in 1955 to 3,179 by 1962, and grew even faster in later

Two AEC diesel railcars outside Oxford loco shed in 1947 – the vehicles are numbers 10 and 11. This part of the shed housed the lifting shop. (Courtesy of R.H.G. Simpson)

The Western class diesel loco *Western Explorer* approaches Aynho Junction on 29 August 1962 with the 15.35 Wolverhampton to Paddington train. (Courtesy of Michael Mensing)

years. At Oxford, the first service to become diesel-powered was the 17.30 fast train to Paddington, with effect from the start of the summer timetable in 1963. The last steam-powered service was on Friday 14 June, when engine number 7018 *Drysllwyn Castle* hauled the 17.30. With driver F. Turner and fireman F. Padley, both of Oxford shed, on the footplate, the train achieved 90mph near Slough, arriving in Paddington early. Next day, the train was hauled by diesel locomotive number D1005 *Western Venturer*.

In spite of various objections, the Beeching cuts began to bite and soon it was the turn of the Cherwell Valley line stations to face the axe. In the event, Tackley, Heyford and Kings Sutton were spared the chop but all the others fell victim. The last stopping trains called at Kidlington, Bletchington, Fritwell & Somerton, Aynho and Fenny Compton on Saturday 31 October 1964. Thereafter, to the rail traveller these places became '... just a group of deserted buildings at the lineside, just a name printed in an out-of-date timetable', commented the *Oxford Mail*. 'The last passengers have gone. The booking office window has slammed shut for the last time. Now the passenger trains speed through'.

The diesel takeover continued unabated and in the summer of 1965 Paddington became a no-go area for steam engines. Interestingly, the last-ever scheduled steam-hauled train to leave was the 16.15 service to Banbury (via the Bicester cut-off) on Friday 11 June. At 18.44 it pulled into Banbury behind engine number 7029 *Clun Castle*, with driver Charles Dudderidge and fireman Alan Bewes, both of Banbury shed, on the footplate. Hordes of enthusiasts debouched onto the platform. Having arrived four minutes late, the driver commented that diesels were cleaner and easier to drive, although the fireman defended 7029. 'She's a good engine', he said, 'and she held her steam very well despite the coal, which is not the right type for the job'.

The end of all Western Region steam haulage was scheduled for the end of November 1965 but in the event it lingered into 1966. The last ever *regular* steam service ran in the Cherwell Valley on Monday 3 January when engine number 6998 *Burton Agnes Hall*, crewed by driver Gerry Faulkener and fireman Pat Cook, came off Oxford shed to take a Poole-York train as far as Banbury. The historic event was made into a civic farewell by inviting the Lord Mayor of Oxford, Ald. Mrs Kathleen Lower, to drive the steam loco from the shed into the platform. Also on the footplate were Mr F.D. Pattisson, London Divisional Manager, and Mr Reginald Hanks, who had retired that weekend after ten years as chairman of the Western Area Board.

At 14.20, after climbing down from the footplate, the mayor waved a green flag to give the 'right away' to the engine crew and 6998 set off. Mrs Lower was allowed to keep the flag as a memento of the occasion, being told 'You'll be able to use it to start council meetings'. 'We'd need a red flag for that', she joked! The mayor was introduced to several railwaymen at Oxford, including shedmaster Joe Trethewey, a Cornishman who had begun his career with the GWR in 1935. His role as shedmaster at Oxford had now ended, as the shed had 'officially' closed on

Coaling engines by hand at Oxford shed, c.1960. This work was typical at the loco sheds and was carried out here until the shed closed in 1965. (Courtesy of R.H.G. Simpson)

31 December 1965. It became a fact with the 'escape' of 6998. (The loco survives at Didcot Railway Centre. The shed was demolished in 1968, becoming a diesel depot until 1984.)

On the Woodford line, the 'Little Banbury' local train had last run on Saturday 13 June 1964, but a service of cross-country passenger trains still used the link line. On the ex-GCR main line, a much reduced service was run. 'Diesel locomotives add to the general despondency', lamented Syd Tyrell, 'no smoke, no fire, not even a decent whistle, more like a blooming ice-cream van'! Even this did not last, however, and on Saturday 3 September 1966, *all* services were withdrawn from the old Great Central route. Syd Tyrell watched the last (steam-hauled) trains leave Woodford station, the 18.40 to Leicester and the 18.50 to Marylebone. He saw two more trains pass through during the night but that was 'the end, the line is now deserted'.

In the Cherwell Valley the final haunt of steam was Banbury shed, which serviced the last few steam engines that strayed into the area until it closed officially on 3 October 1966 (becoming a diesel depot until 1984). On 16 June, for instance, number 7029 *Clun Castle* (officially withdrawn at the end of 1965) came here, having helped out on a Bordesley-Banbury freight train. During the twilight of steam, Banbury's shed became a 'locomotive abattoir' where dozens of steam engines were cut up by scrap merchant James Friswell Ltd, but *Clun Castle* was 'one that got away'. In private ownership, it hauled a Paddington-Birkenhead train on part of its journey on 4 March 1967. (It is now preserved at Birmingham Railway Museum.)

That weekend was an ominous occasion, for it marked the end of express services on the Western Region's line to the north. The last main line train, on Sunday 5 March 1967, was the 21.40 Birkenhead-Paddington. Local trains still ran on the ex-GWR 'Northern' route via Birmingham (Snow Hill), until Birkenhead (Woodside) station was closed with effect from Saturday 4 November 1967. All links from the Birkenhead area into Paddington were severed after 1 March 1968, when work also began on reducing the Bicester 'cut-off' to a single track between Aynho and Princes Risborough. Between 1961 and 1969, Dr Beeching halved British Railways' route mileage and axed 4,000 stations. The GWR's Snow Hill station closed on 6 March 1972.

From now on, the ex-LNWR line from Euston became the primary route to the north-west via Birmingham, where trains used New Street station. Trains on the ex-GWR 'Northern' line were diverted into it. In a sense, the GWR lost to the LNWR in the 'Battle of the Gauges' thanks to Dr Beeching! Moreover, trains using the Bicester 'cut-off' were also diverted, from Paddington to the ex-GCR terminus at Marylebone. British Rail was itself doomed from 1994, when privatization replaced national ownership in the biggest shake-up of rail transport since 1947. When all was said and done though, trains still ran on the Cherwell Valley railway. While only a shadow of its former self, it had survived, having witnessed many comings and goings in its chequered history!

# 18   Kidlington: a case study

The rise and fall of Kidlington station closely mirrors the changing fortunes of the Cherwell Valley railway as a whole and it is certainly instructive to put it 'under the microscope'. Some of the things which have already been written about it in secondary sources are vague or incorrect but careful scrutiny of the primary sources available clarifies most of the issues.

Kidlington, the first station on the railway north of Oxford, did not open at the same time as the line, nor was it originally named 'Kidlington'. Indeed, it was not actually intended to serve the village of that name at all, but rather the town of Woodstock, which already had a station!

During construction of the Oxford & Rugby Railway, issues arising from land purchases by the railway company were dealt with at Kidlington's parish vestry meetings. In May, 1847, it was resolved that the poor rates of local farms be adjusted in the light of land purchases made by the GWR. Then, in September, it was resolved to seek £100 from the company for a 'rood' of land 'adjacent to the turnpike road' at the Langford Lane gravel pit. In June 1848, after some litigation, the GWR actually paid the parish £60 for the land and in March 1849 the vestry resolved to spend the money on improving footpaths around the village.

The GWR, meanwhile, was busy changing the topography of the northern tip of the parish. Before the railway came here the 'Oxford-Adderbury turnpike road' (it remained so until 1876) only crossed the canal on a small stone-arch bridge built in 1788. To cross the new railway, the navvies built a large three-span skew bridge consisting of two side brick-arch spans, each of 18ft 5in, and a central cast-iron arched-girder span of 37ft. The outer brick retaining walls were two feet thick at their base and contained 16ft of filling. The abutments of the centre arch were each erected on two-foot-deep 'rafts' of lime concrete. This was a solid bridge!

At the same time, the existing canal bridge was widened for road traffic on its eastern side by the addition of a cast-iron girder 'trough'. However, the road between the canal and railway bridges formed a severe S-bend, and a canal-side cottage on the north bank obscured visibility. Worse, to clear the railway line under the new bridge, the GWR raised the road level some 10ft and increased the approach gradients accordingly. Thus by November 1848, as well as the old 'awkward corner', there was now 'a considerable hill to mount', because the GWR had economised on 'the expense of carting a little more of their rubbish to the fillings'.

As construction of the line neared completion, in November 1849, the inhabitants campaigned for a railway station in the parish. 'A petition is being got up in this village', *Jackson's Oxford Journal* reported, 'as well as in Woodstock, to the Directors of the Great Western Railway Company, praying them to fix on Langford-lane (sic), in the parish of Kidlington, as a site for the first station out of Oxford'. The next month, the GWR advertised in the local press for tenders from

Kidlington station frontage, *c.*1964. Built around 1855, the down side building seen here survived the Beeching axe but was severely damaged by fire in 1990.

contractors interested in various jobs including building 'the minor stations on the Oxford and Rugby Railway'. This time round, however, Kidlington's was not one of them.

A station named 'Woodstock' (located near Bletchingdon) did open in September 1850 at the same time as the line from Oxford to Banbury. Nevertheless, work was soon in hand on erecting a station by the bridge at Langford Lane, on land which is described in the *Book of Reference* of the Oxford & Rugby Railway as belonging to the Duke of Marlborough and being 'allotments laid out in gardens'. The company's cashbooks show payments in 1854-1855 of over £2,000 to contractor Edward Streeter, for constructing the station buildings, and various sums to Messrs Orton & Child in 1855 for constructing the station yard and sidings.

The opening was somewhat deferred: 'The disappointment at not opening the Kidlington station on the GWR, which was fully expected on 1st May, has been sensibly felt by many persons', stated the *Oxford Chronicle*, adding, 'As the station has been erected nearly two years, it is not easy to conceive what can be the motive for witholding the so much desired accommodation from the public'. It opened at last on Friday 1 June 1855. 'It is designated in the June time-bills as the *Woodstock Road Station*' reported *Jackson's Oxford Journal*. The station known until then by that name would henceforth be designated Kirtlington station.

Built of Cotswold stone in typical Brunel style, it was a two-platform wayside station. Its main passenger accommodation was reached via an approach road from the turnpike but was on the platform furthest away from Kidlington village. This reflected the fact (as the GWR explicitly advertised) that it was 'a new station for Woodstock'. Nevertheless, Kidlington's vestry promptly rated the new station at £30! Philip Slatter, landlord of the King's Arms Hotel, Woodstock, equally promptly took over the Railway Hotel (previously known as The Anchor) close by, advertising 'every accommodation – Post Horses, Flys, and other vehicles'.

It would appear that some travellers still preferred such transport. Commenting on the new station, the *Oxford Chronicle* said that 'the parishioners do not esteem the accommodation so much as was anticipated owing to the fare being nearly double from what it used to be by the other conveyances (it being about 2d. a mile)'. Unless there was a reduction, travellers would 'mostly continue to use the old routes to and from Oxford'. But the new station – served by five 'down' and four 'up' stopping trains daily (three each way on Sundays) – was profitable, as is indicated by the fact that its rateable value was increased by 50% in 1856.

Along with the passenger facilities, the station had a cattle dock, yard and sidings. Within a few years of its opening, a 57ft by 40ft goods shed was built in the yard. Of typical broad-gauge design, it had separate road and rail vehicle entrances, a central transfer platform with a 30cwt manual crane, and offices. Freight traffic from Kidlington included consignments of livestock, vegetables and fruit from local farms. At this date, the village produced large crops of apples, plums and apricots, which were transported by rail to markets in Oxford and London: 'Kidlington yearly sent up to Covent Garden Market 6000 dozen apricots'.

From the village direction pedestrian access to the station was via a footpath which led down to the north end of the Oxford-bound platform. To reach the

A general view of Kidlington station looking south, *c.*1960, showing the main line and branch bay platforms – the stationmaster's house can just be seen on the left. (Courtesy of the *Oxford Mail*)

Kidlington signal box looking north up the track, *c.*1960. This signal box was built in 1890 and demolished around 1968. (Courtesy of Nigel Payne)

Banbury-bound platform there was a foot crossing over the rails until a footbridge was built in 1890. Initially, train movements were controlled by 'bobbies', or railway 'policemen', who roamed the tracks in the vicinity of the station, turning the 'boards' (the GWR disc-and-crossbar signals) and changing the points as required. Later, a signal box was built on the 'down' platform around 1883, to be superseded by one on the 'up' line beyond the road bridge in around 1890.

The names and service dates of Kidlington's stationmasters over the years can be gleaned from the registers of *GWR Company Servants*, although precisely who was the first is not clear. A thorough search shows that a new stationmaster was appointed at the original Woodstock Road (Bletchingdon) station in November 1854 and he may also have had responsibility for the new Woodstock Road (Kidlington) station when that opened some months later. This was William Evans Trigg, (who later became Banbury's stationmaster). At exactly the same date that he was promoted (May 1860), another appointment was made at Kidlington.

The new man at Kidlington was Thomas Hardie, appointed stationmaster in May 1860 at a salary of £80 per year. Sadly, he died in service at the age of just twenty-eight in August 1862. Then came Royston Steadman, just nineteen years old, but he was 'dismissed' by the GWR in November 1862. Next was Humphrey Brown, who served until March 1863, going on on to become stationmaster at Banbury, from where (in 1866) he 'absconded' with the takings! (To cover this eventuality, stationmasters had to take out sureties with the GWR Guarantee Fund). He was followed by John Rengger, who served here until 'dismissed' in September 1868.

Frederick Bell was Kidlington's 'much respected station master'. Although apparently born in London, he had joined the GWR as goods clerk at Oxford in July 1858, being promoted to passenger clerk in August 1862. In May 1864 he was appointed as stationmaster at Aynho (incidentally, succeeding Hubert Simmons) and then at Kidlington in September 1868. With his wife and three children, he lived at Hill Cottage in High Street. His salary was increased to £90 in February 1874, but he had to cope with the 'frightful smash' at Hampton Gay at Christmas in that year. Aged just thirty-three years, he 'resigned' from the GWR in March 1876.

Kidlington's subsequent stationmasters included William Dyment, who served exactly a year here, then Albert Cook (from February to December, 1877), David Thomas (to January, 1879), who went on to become Cheltenham stationmaster, Henry Tidbury (to January 1881), William Golby (to February 1883), Frederick Dodds (to February 1886) and Elias Cordrey (to September 1888). Then came Albert Lofting. He had joined the GWR at Oxford as a telegraph boy in 1877 and served as stationmaster at Kidlington until June 1890, going on to take the stationmaster's post at Woodstock until 1894 (being succeeded there by Thomas Ashford) and then at Starcross and Lostwithiel.

Signalman Ivor Betteridge in the signal box, March 1963. The box was manned in three eight-hour shifts at this date, Ivor sharing them with signalmen Wally Franklin and Gilbert Holder. (Courtesy of the *Oxford Mail*)

Upon the opening of the Woodstock branch in 1890, Kidlington's station ceased to be known as 'Woodstock Road' and instead became 'Kidlington – change for Blenheim & Woodstock'. On becoming a junction station, the layout of the original wayside station was considerably modifed. Northward extensions were added to the two existing platforms, creating a 325ft 'up' platform and a 572ft 'down' platform, behind which there was a 298ft bay platform for branch trains. A stationmaster's house was built and the main platforms were linked by a footbridge. As originally built, the footbridge had a covering canopy but this was removed in about 1936.

A new signal box was constructed north of the road bridge on the 'up' side of the line. Built of brick and timber, it measured 31ft 9in by 11ft 6in, with a floor 8ft above rail-level. Thomas Blackall, the GWR signalling engineer, installed much new signal inter-locking equipment, at a cost to the company of £1,285. Secondary sources differ as to its nature, but a Plan dated 5 February 1889 shows that it consisted of a signal frame with a total of forty-six levers, comprising 'signal levers – 17; disc – 11; point – 7; facing point lock – 5; spare – 6'. Similarly, at the time of Colonel Yorke's inspection in 1900, the signal box was reported to have just forty-six levers.

From June 1890, Kidlington's stationmaster was William Thomas Cooke. He began his GWR career as a porter at Oxford, in which capacity he served elsewhere on the system before being appointed to Kidlington at a wage of 30s per week. The GWR 'fined' him four times – twice for 'neglect of duty' – between 1886 and 1893, but 'commended' him in 1911. He lived in the station house with his wife and his daughters, Florence and Winifred, becoming Kidlington's longest serving stationmaster by working here until his retirement at the age of sixty-five in May 1927. He died, aged seventy-two, on 11 March 1935 and is buried at Wolvercote cemetery.

William Cooke presided at Kidlington throughout the station's heyday. In its 'Edwardian Summer' numerous passenger trains came through daily, both express and local, along with two dozen goods trains, mostly at night, including a few 'pick-up' goods trains which shunted wagons here. At this date, the staff still found time to work on the station gardens, turning them into some of the finest on the GWR. From 1904 the Directors offered 'ordinary' and 'special' prizes for the best station garden in each of the principal divisions of the line and Kidlington won on a number of occasions, winning £5 special prizes in both 1911 and 1913.

Kidlington was a fairly busy station. In peacetime, its busiest year was 1913, when 16,537 tickets were sold (representing an average of forty-five passengers a day), producing £788 in revenue. With £352 from parcel traffic plus £1,781 from goods and livestock (based on 4,828 tons of goods and 119 livestock wagons), total station receipts were £2,921 for the year. By contrast, Kidlington's wages bill that year was only £507, which paid for a total of ten staff, comprising one stationmaster (class 4 out of 9 grades), one general clerk, two porters, three signalmen and three crossing keepers – at the Roundham, Sandy Lane and Yarnton level crossings.

To create more business the GWR encouraged firms to locate near its stations. At Kidlington the company owned land around the station which it let on lease, such as the Railway Hotel 'with the coach house, stables, cattle pens, pigsties, outbuildings, yard, gardens and premises', which was leased to Hall's Oxford Brewery in 1909, having 'for some years past been in the occupation of the Lessees'. A timber yard had been created behind the hotel and adjacent to the station yard by 1880 and it prospered under various lessees. William H. Branch, 'Timber & Firewood Merchant', traded here from 1896 until well after the First World War.

In 1922 the GWR leased a plot of land behind the timber yard to the Alden Engine Company of Oxford but the firm went into receivership without being able to build its proposed factory and gave up the lease in 1924. In 1923 the Oxfordshire Farmers' Bacon Factory started production here and had more success. The Duke of York (later King George VI) and his wife visited it in 1924 and in 1936 it was taken over by C & T Harris Ltd. In 1927 the Oxford & Shipton Cement Company was established and in 1929 began production at a new works near Shipton. Extensive railway sidings were put in and all the cement was taken away by rail.

After William Cooke retired in May 1927 he was followed by Harry Pinnock, who stayed until October, 1930, being succeeded by John Jones. Then, in 1937, came Jesse Silman. As part of the GWR's economy drive, all three of them doubled as stationmasters at Woodstock too. By the latter date, traffic on the Oxford-Banbury road was growing. It had increased by 78% since 1931. To cope with the extra traffic, the road bridge over the railway had been widened in 1925 and its cast-iron girders replaced with steel ones but now Oxfordshire County Council decided to build a replacement bridge, along with others, including one over the nearby canal.

Construction of the new bridge was undertaken in two sections so that the road could be kept open to traffic, which was controlled from a tall wooden cabin, with a man inside operating a 'stop-go' sign. Demolition of the eastern side of the old bridge started on 18 May 1937 and three new steel frames were erected on 11 July. Prefabricated at Chepstow, they were brought to the site by rail and lifted into place by a GWR thirty-six-ton mobile crane. This section was opened to traffic on 2 November and demolition of the western side then began. By 30 June 1938 the new 79ft 8in single-span steel and concrete bridge was ready for normal traffic.

During the Second World War, from 1940, Woodstock was given its own stationmaster again and Jesse Silman was solely responsible for Kidlington. In the war years, the station saw its heaviest traffic ever. Between 1939 and 1944, ticket sales jumped from 5,531 to 22,373 and freight from 4,167 to 11,942 tons. In 1947, Jesse Silman was succeeded by Frederick Needle, who was followed in 1956 by C.R. Hall. Then, in January 1959, David Owen became Kidlington's last stationmaster. He had started his railway career at Fishguard and – being just twenty-six when he came to Kidlington – was reputed to be the youngest stationmaster in the country.

Horse Guards arrived by rail for the Royal Show in 1960. They are seenleaving the station yard by the 'approach road' for the nearby airfield. (Courtesy of the late D.E. Owen)

Stationmaster David Owen in the booking office at Kidlington station, March 1963. When appointed in 1959, he was reputed to be the youngest stationmaster in the country. (Courtesy of the *Oxford Mail*)

Sadly, the station was by now in a state of terminal decline. When it opened a century earlier, Kidlington had a population of less than 1,500. This had grown to around 12,000 but the station did not benefit: in 1959, only 3,217 tickets were sold (representing an average of some eight passengers a day), although 5,567 tons of goods were handled. The Royal Agricultural Show was held at the nearby airfield in 1960, creating much special rail traffic (including the arrival of the Royal Horse Artillery) but it was short-lived. Reporting on the Beeching plan in 1963, the *Oxford Mail* named the local stations to be axed and Kidlington was on the list.

'Kidlington station stood deserted as its death sentence was announced', it was reported. 'A heavy drizzle added to the gloomy atmosphere'. Under the headline 'One station that couldn't keep up', David Owen was quoted as saying that there was no future for passenger traffic at the station. The half-dozen trains each way from the station could not compete with the frequent bus service and growth in car ownership. Eventually, it was announced that, like most other stations on the Oxford-Banbury line, Kidlington would close on Monday 2 November 1964. As there was no Sunday service, closure took effect on the Saturday before.

Perhaps appropriately, the last ever passenger trains called at Kidlington station on 31 October – Hallowe'en. In the early darkness of an autumn evening, the 16.40 Wolverhampton-Didcot local paused briefly at 19.00. Ten minutes later the 17.44 Reading-Banbury local really was the final train to stop by. Both trains were diesel multiple units. As they growled away, there was no ceremony On the platform, watching their tail lights disappear into the dark night, there were just two teenage train-spotters with David Owen (who completed his career on the railway at Oxford). After 109 years, Kidlington had seen its last passenger trains.

It was not quite the end, as the station remained open for parcels and goods until 1 March 1965. Thereafter, the platforms and up side station buildings were demolished, although the down side buildings were retained and used commercially. The footbridge was carefully dismantled in October 1965 and re-erected at Didcot (to replace a similar bridge which had been destroyed by a fire, after a petrol train crashed into it in August 1964). Kidlington's signal box, along with the goods loop vestiges of the branch, was taken out of use on 16 September 1968 and later demolished. The Brunelian goods shed survived these but was finally demolished in 1984.

In 1967, even the erstwhile Railway Hotel was re-named the Wise Alderman (after Alderman Frank Wise) though there is still a railway connection as he worked in Kidlington signal box for many years. The remaining station building lay empty and became subject to vandalism. It was badly damaged by fire on the evening of 6 August 1990, but as a Grade II listed building the derelict remains cannot be demolished. Although various proposals have been made to open a new station at Kidlington, the favoured site is at Park Farm, so the old station site will not be used. A pity really, since it has witnessed more than a century of Kidlington's history.

# Acknowledgements

I am grateful to the following for their kindness in loaning or granting reproduction rights for their photographs to be used in this book: Mr Ken Ashton, Mr David Canning (D.E. Canning Railway Photography), Mrs Rosemary Giraud, Mr Michael Mensing, Mr Ron Morbey, Mr Nigel Oram (Kingfisher Postcards), the late Mr David Owen, the *Oxford Mail*, Mr Nigel Payne, Mr R.H.G. Simpson, Mr John Smith (Lens of Sutton). Thanks also to Dr Pamela Horn for permission to reproduce extracts from *The Diaries of George James Dew*.

# Bibliography

*Cherwell Valley Railway* has been written as a social history of the railway line based largely on research conducted in primary sources, particularly contemporary newspaper reports in publications such as *Jackson's Oxford Journal*, the *Oxford Times*, the *Oxford Mail* and the *Banbury Guardian*. However, the following secondary sources have been consulted and used where appropriate to place local developments within a national context. They may be of interest to the general reader who wishes to investigate certain matters in more detail.

| | |
|---|---|
| Alves, John | 'Resorts for Railfans – 29:Oxford', *Trains Illustrated*, 1959 |
| Booker, Frank | *The Great Western Railway*, David & Charles, 1977 |
| Coleman, Terry | *The Railway Navvies*, Penguin, 1968 |
| Compton, H.J. | *The Oxford Canal*, David & Charles, 1976 |
| Davies, R. and Grant, M. | *Forgotten Railways of the Cotswolds and Chilterns*, David & Charles, 1975 |
| Eckersley, R. | 'Oxford – An Operational Problem', *Railway Magazine*, 1954 |
| Ellis, C.H. | *The Royal Trains*, Routledge & Kegan Paul, 1975 |
| Emery, Frank | *The Oxfordshire Landscape*, Hodder & Stoughton, 1974 |
| Fasnacht, Ruth | *A History of the City of Oxford*, Basil Blackwell, 1954 |
| Horn, Pamela | *The Diaries of George James Dew* (two vols), Beacon Publications, 1983 and 1986 |
| Jenkins, Stanley | *The Woodstock Branch*, Wild Swan, 1987 |
| Lingard, Richard | *The Woodstock Branch*, Oxford Publishing Company, 1973 |
| MacDermot, E.T. | *History of the Great Western Railway* (two vols), 1927, Ian Allan reprint 1974 |
| Parkes, G.D. | 'The Woodstock Branch', *Railway Magazine*, 1952 |
| Potts, William | *A History of Banbury*, Banbury Guardian, 1958 |
| Rolt, L.T.C. | *Red For Danger*, Pan Books, 1960 |
| Russell, J.H. | *The Banbury and Cheltenham Railway*, Oxford Publishing Company, 1977 |
| Simmons, Ernest | *Memoirs of a Station Master*, Adams & Dart, 1879, reprinted 1974 |
| Simmons, Jack | *The Railways of Britain*, Macmillan, 1968 |
| Smith, D.N. | *The Railway and its Passengers*, David & Charles, 1988 |
| Trinder, Barrie | *Victorian Banbury*, Phillimore, 1982 |
| Tyrrell, Syd | *A Countryman's Tale*, Constable, 1973 |
| Semmens, P.W.B. | *The Great Western Railway, 1939-1948*, Allen & Unwin, 1985 |
| Stapleton, B | *Three Oxfordshire Parishes*, Clarendon Press, 1893 |
| Vaughan, Adrian | *Grime and Glory*, John Murray, 1985 |
| Vaughan, Adrian | *The Great Western at Work, 1921-1939*, Patrick Stephens, 1993 |